HARRY STYLES

Also by Sean Smith

Meghan Misunderstood
Spice Girls
Ed Sheeran
George
Adele
Kim
Tom Jones: The Life
Kylie
Gary
Alesha
Tulisa
Kate
Robbie
Cheryl
Victoria
Justin: The Biography
Britney: The Biography
J.K. Rowling: A Biography
Jennifer: The Unauthorized Biography
Royal Racing
The Union Game
Sophie's Kiss (with Garth Gibbs)
Stone Me! (with Dale Lawrence)

HARRY STYLES

THE MAKING OF A MODERN MAN

BY SEAN SMITH

SUNDAY TIMES BESTSELLING AUTHOR

HarperCollins*Publishers*

HarperCollins*Publishers*
1 London Bridge Street
London SE1 9GF

www.harpercollins.co.uk

HarperCollins*Publishers*
1st Floor, Watermarque Building, Ringsend Road
Dublin 4, Ireland

First published by HarperCollins*Publishers* 2021

1 3 5 7 9 10 8 6 4 2

© Sean Smith 2021

Sean Smith asserts the moral right to be
identified as the author of this work

A catalogue record of this book is
available from the British Library

HB ISBN 978-0-00-835952-2
TPB ISBN 978-0-00-835955-3

Printed and bound in the UK using 100%
renewable electricity at CPI Group (UK) Ltd

MIX
Paper from
responsible sources
FSC
www.fsc.org
FSC™ C007454

This book is produced from independently certified FSC™ paper
to ensure responsible forest management.

For more information visit: www.harpercollins.co.uk/green

To Joma –
wishing you a wonderful future

'… If you are black, if you are white, if you are gay, if you are straight, if you are transgender – whoever you are, whoever you want to be – I support you. I love every single one of you.'

Harry Styles, Ericsson Globe, Stockholm, 18 March 2018

CONTENTS

———

PART THREE:
A MODERN MAN

FIRST IMPRESSIONS

———

It wasn't the eye-catching cover of *Vogue* that did it for me. It wasn't the envy-making cavorting with beautiful people on an idyllic, sun-kissed Malibu beach for the video of 'Watermelon Sugar'; it wasn't two number one albums or his role in *Dunkirk*.

No, what triggered a fascination with Harry Styles and made me want to write a book about him were just a few words from the actor and director Olivia Wilde, who described him as 'very modern', and observed, 'I hope that this brand of confidence as a male that Harry has — truly devoid of any traces of toxic masculinity — is indicative of his generation and therefore the future of the world.'

Wow, that's quite an endorsement of a man who just ten years earlier had done his best to impress Simon Cowell with a version of Stevie Wonder's sentimental chestnut 'Isn't She Lovely'. Did he deserve such praise from Olivia, I wonder?

Like fifteen million others I had watched the entire seventh series of *The X Factor* in the days when it was compulsory Saturday night viewing. You literally weren't part of the Sunday conversation if you hadn't seen Matt, Rebecca, Cher and the boys from One Direction battle it out every week to stay in the competition.

The five members of One Direction had sparkle and youthful exuberance, but I had no idea they were going to rule the pop world in such a short space of time. The stars aligned for them: the world was ready for a new boy band; they had a brilliant team looking after them day to day and they had the unswerving support of the corporate board room where careers were made or broken.

The boys were only together for five intense, mad years – becoming multi-millionaires – before going on indefinite hiatus in December 2015. With a few exceptions, five years seems to be the average life span of a boy or girl band – especially one put together by a third party. That was true of Take That and the Spice Girls, for example.

Zayn Malik had left One Direction before the official hiatus, which was a nice way of describing a full stop. Harry, though, was already looking different from the others. He had longer rock-star hair and an eye for the fashionable and flamboyant.

But nice hair and the ability to look good in a Gucci suit did not make him modern. My task in this book is to see if the description of Harry Styles as a modern man is justified. Is Olivia right or is referencing toxic masculinity just a neat soundbite? You don't just arrive ready-made as a beacon of the present and future, so who are the friends, the role models and the influencers that have helped Harry on his journey? And what does it actually mean to be 'modern' anyway?

These are the questions I hope to answer in a serious look at a superstar: *Harry Styles: The Making of a Modern Man*. See you on the other side …

PART ONE

FINDING
DIRECTION

1

DRESSING UP

———

Harry Styles was nearly born in the back of a car. His dad, Des, confessed that he and his heavily pregnant wife, Anne, only just made it to the Alexandra Hospital in Redditch before their son was on his way. It was a twenty-mile dash up the A46 in Worcestershire from their home in Evesham. There wasn't even time to 'call the midwife'. Instead, Harry Edward Styles said hello to the world at 2am on 1 February 1994.

There's a memorial statue in Redditch that honours a very famous name in world music. But it's not Harry. Instead, pride of place in the town centre belongs to John Bonham, the legendary drummer with Led Zeppelin.

The local papers and media always refer to Harry as Redditch-born whenever the more-recent superstar does anything noteworthy, but in reality he has no connection with the town half an hour south of Birmingham other than noting it as his place of birth on the official paperwork.

A month after his second birthday, the Styles family moved. Des and Anne sold the three-bedroom semi-detached house in St Philips Drive, Evesham, an estate close to the main road, and relocated a hundred miles north to rural Cheshire. They were a family of four: Harry had an elder sister, Gemma, who was three when he was born.

They settled into a spacious four-bedroom house in Chestnut Drive, Holmes Chapel, a large village that enjoyed a rural atmosphere despite being close to the motorway, and an easy twenty-mile commute into Manchester. The town of Crewe was even closer – just eight miles south.

If there is going to be a statue of Harry Styles in the future then it should be in Holmes Chapel, probably in the main square near St Luke's Church, or there's plenty of room outside his local secondary school in Selkirk Drive. Harry once said that nothing much happened in Holmes Chapel. That may be true, but it's not a sleepy village and these days it is a bustling place, more like a small town than the gentle setting for an Agatha Christie whodunit or an episode of *Midsomer Murders*.

The proximity to Manchester was ideal for Harry's dad, who was a committed supporter of Manchester United, and these were the best of times for the club enjoying the glory years of Alex Ferguson and a first team that included Eric Cantona, Roy Keane, Paul Scholes and David Beckham. There was always plenty of football memorabilia dotted around the Styles' house. At the time, Des, who was ten years older than his then 28-year-old wife, worked in financial services as an operational manager for HFC bank, primarily responsible for arranging loans and credit.

Anne had her hands full with two young children. They could scarcely have been more different. Harry's elder sister was the quiet, studious one, an A-grade student throughout school who found the academic side of things much easier than standing up in front of the class, and could only look on a little jealously as her cheeky and precociously charismatic kid brother sailed through life.

Harry did secure an A once, for his very first English essay, and he was proud of his achievement – but perhaps the top mark lived long in his memory because it was all downhill from there and he never matched it. He was always the boy getting told off by the teacher for chatting away to his friends at the back of the class.

His first pre-school nursery was called, sweetly, Happy Days, and it was just two minutes' walk from their detached house in Chestnut Drive, a smart new-build with a large garden for their dog, Max, to patrol. He was a cross between a border collie and a lurcher, who could sometimes look a bit fierce but wasn't, and he loved the children to bits. Gemma had chosen him from a litter because he was the outsider – the only puppy who was not pure black.

Ironically Harry's very first word was not dog but 'cat'. Anne had driven the children to visit their grandparents, Brian and Mary Selley, in Hampshire. As they were walking up the path to the front door, the family feline appeared. Little Harry pointed and declared 'cat', which made everyone's day.

When he was old enough, Harry joined his sister round the corner at the Hermitage Primary School. As was usual on these occasions, Mum came too to make sure her five-year-old was going to be alright. She sat in the class for an hour or so before slipping away. Harry may have been a bit of a 'mummy's boy', as Anne has always affectionately said, but she didn't leave a child weeping and wailing for his mother. He settled down to enjoy the day until she was back to walk him and Gemma home.

From a young age Harry was one of the boys *and* one of the girls. He never seemed limited by gender stereotyping or, as he memorably put it, 'I wasn't one of those boys who thought girls were smelly.' Just to prove it he gave one little girl, Phoebe, a teddy bear as a present when they were six.

Right from the start, Harry was an enthusiastic performer in the school plays, confident enough, it seemed, to get up on stage and sing, whatever embarrassing costume he had to wear. For the Christmas musical in December 2000, he played the title role of Barney, a church mouse; he sported a pair of Gemma's grey tights, a headband with oversized ears sticking out the top and a long string tail. Looking back on his starring role aged six, he observed, 'I like to think I was a good mouse.'

Often, enthusiastic mums can light the fire for their children – perhaps taking them to dance classes or booking piano lessons before they could barely walk. Anne loved playing dressing-up games with her children, painstakingly making elaborate papier-mâché outfits, including one that featured Harry as the World Cup. He also had a *101 Dalmatians* outfit, which was a particular favourite and the one he wore all the time around the house. Anne explained, 'I was always a big fan of doing fancy dress when my children were small … which Gemma hated but Harry always embraced.'

Harry would carry his love of dressing up into adulthood, and in his now-famous *Vogue* interview in 2020 he acknowledged, 'There's so much joy to be had in playing with clothes. I've never thought too much about what it means – it just becomes this extended part of creating something.'

In the primary school favourite, *Chitty Chitty Bang Bang*, he played Buzz Lightyear, who obviously did not feature in the original musical. In his school's adaptation, the children hid from the scary Child Catcher in a toy store where Buzz and Woody from *Toy Story* were living.

Harry also played the Pharaoh in a production of *Joseph and the Amazing Technicolor Dreamcoat*. The character's big number is 'Song of the King' and he delivered it as if Elvis Presley had been transported back to biblical times. The first pop song that Harry learned all the words to was 'Girl of My Best Friend', a number that 'the King' originally recorded for his 1960 UK number 1 album *Elvis is Back*. The track was one of his dad's favourites.

None of the family was especially musical, but Des at least loved a wide variety of past and present records and his son grew up hugely influenced by not just Elvis but also The Beatles and Coldplay – not forgetting a smattering of Fleetwood Mac and the peerless 'Shine on You Crazy Diamond' by Pink Floyd, the epic tribute to the band's original lead singer, Syd Barrett.

Harry was able to practise his inner rock star with the help of a karaoke machine his grandpa Brian had bought him for Christmas. Harry remained particularly close to Brian over the years, describing the man who picked him up and told him to be brave when he fell over and scraped his knee as 'the coolest guy ever'.

The admiration was mutual: recalling his grandson as a small boy, Brian observed that he always had a smile on his face.

The famous smile left Harry completely, however, one dreadful evening when he was seven and his parents sat him and Gemma down in the lounge and told them gently that they were splitting up. Everyone was in tears. Des later recalled, movingly, 'It was the worst day of my life. Harry wasn't a cry baby or generally emotional but he cried then.'

Although Des and Anne had agreed to separate, he didn't move out immediately, which perhaps made the situation a little easier for their children. There was even a memorable family summer holiday to Cyprus when Harry, according to both his father and his sister, became the mascot of the teenage girls at the resort hotel. While Gemma was a bit of a loner, Harry was the centre of attention around the pool, entertaining everyone with his now-trademark cheeky grin and boisterous nature.

To Des's astonishment, when it came for them to leave on the shuttle bus to the airport, a crowd of young women gathered to wave goodbye to his young son. 'Bye, Harry, we love you,' they shouted as the bus sped away. 'He's very charming,' said Des, simply.

Eventually, and inevitably, Des moved out of the family home and the divorce was finalised. He still saw the children every couple of weeks, doing his best to make sure everything was alright with both of them, supporting them financially and, when he could, with any emotional problems.

Des was not a million miles away, moving to the outskirts of Manchester. 'I'm not an estranged dad,' he said, and he wasn't, as would prove to be very much the case in the future. He was always close enough to take his son to football or buy him a club jersey or two for the bedroom wall.

Anne, meanwhile, met someone, a man who really would become estranged from them in the future – in his case, a future stepfather. John Cox was the good-looking landlord of the Red Lion pub in Pickmere, a village twenty minutes' drive past the town of Northwich.

Anne was a vivaciously attractive woman of thirty-three when they met, although they didn't start going out until they had known each other for a year. They were soon making plans for a life together, setting a wedding date for April 2003, not long after Harry's ninth birthday.

They chose a swish local venue, the Mere Golf Club – now the Mere Golf Resort and Spa but still known in this part of rural Cheshire as 'The Mere'. For the big day, Harry looked immaculate in a dress suit complete with a black bow tie, an early indication of a young man who was born to wear a suit well. After the wedding, Harry and Gemma were dropped off at Des's to allow the newlyweds to jet off to Mauritius for their honeymoon.

Before the celebration, the happy couple had already joined forces to take over the Antrobus Arms, a large country pub on the main A558 Warrington Road. The premises formerly run by Lancashire brewers Greenall Whitley needed a lot of work, so they set about the refurbishment and decorating to turn it into a sparkling new local for the village of Antrobus. It was a large building, so it made economic sense for the new landlord and landlady to live upstairs with Harry and Gemma.

John and Anne didn't want to lose the feel of a traditional Cheshire pub, making sure the Antrobus Arms retained a tap room and a back room where charities and societies could hold evening events. Half a mile away was the Antrobus post office, run by two regulars at the pub, Trevor and Sandra

Collins. They became firm friends of Anne in particular. They also had a son, Reg, who was nearer Gemma's age but was Harry's best buddy when the family moved into the pub.

Harry stayed at the Hermitage Primary School in Holmes Chapel but during the holidays he was pleased to have a good friend nearby. They went on long bike rides together, exploring the country lanes but always making sure they popped in for a cornet on the way home at the Ice Cream Farm in Great Budworth, two miles away.

The parlour, run by June Wilkinson and her family, is one of the hidden gems of this part of rural Cheshire, but once discovered it becomes a habit that's hard to break, as was the case with Harry when he discovered their christmas pudding flavour one chilly December afternoon.

Even more important than ice cream, Harry started having informal guitar lessons when he was ten from a pub regular who had once been in a rock band. Harry has never shouted about his early musical training but it gave him a start that would be valuable when he picked up a guitar as a career musician and songwriter.

Harry seemed to settle in well to life at the pub, although he was notorious in the household for being untidy. He sang in public for the first time – apart from performing in school plays – when he joined John at The Elms, another pub in Pickmere. When John got up to sing, Harry insisted he join him and the pair gave a rousing rendition of 'New York, New York', the Frank Sinatra favourite.

For the moment, though, Harry was more interested in sport than crooning. He enjoyed badminton, taking it up because his dad played. He was also keen on football, playing for a boys' team on a Sunday, although he was never going to be signed up by a United scout.

John Cox completely disappeared out of Harry's life when he and Anne split up in 2006. He is no longer part of the Harry Styles story and hasn't seen him since Anne moved back to Holmes Chapel. He has been erased from the family history. Neither Harry, his mother nor his sister have ever mentioned him, although Anne continued to be known as Anne Cox right up to the heady days of *The X Factor*.

John was eventually tracked down by the investigative journalist Sharon Feinstein. He was still living in Cheshire but was no longer in the pub business. He spoke warmly of Harry and hoped that one day they might meet up for a drink.

In the small world of this part of Cheshire, the Antrobus Arms was sold to Trevor and Sandra Collins, who would keep up the tradition of a thriving country pub for the next twelve years One of the regulars was a local businessman called Robin Twist, a sociable and popular chap who would be a significant figure in Harry's life in the years to come.

Anne, meanwhile, bought a modest three-bedroom terraced house in London Road, Holmes Chapel, within walking distance of the local comprehensive school. Harry would soon be a teenager.

2

WHITE ESKIMO DAYS

Harry's football career was not going well. He was playing for the Holmes Chapel Hurricanes FC, a junior team set up in 2000 by local businessman Chris Rogers so that his son and his friends could enjoy a game on weekends. According to Chris, Harry wasn't the most physical of players, although he did score a few goals.

The lowest point of his footballing days, however, was when he had to stand in for the regular goalkeeper. The Hurricanes lost the game 8–0. He wasn't asked to play in that position again. The plus side of his weekly ordeal was that the mums and sisters on the touchline were always charmed by Harry, who was quick with a little quip to cheer up everyone.

He may not have impressed with his soccer skills but at least he was having fun with his mates away from school. One in particular, Will Sweeny, would be a significant friend. Will was the closest thing to a celebrity at Holmes Chapel Comprehensive School because his mum, Yvette Fielding, was a familiar face on television.

Yvette had been the presenter of *Blue Peter* when she was just eighteen and subsequently appeared in a host of TV programmes, including as the presenter of the cult show *Most Haunted*, which also featured her second husband, Karl Beattie. They lived on a farm not far from Holmes Chapel. Harry was a regular visitor after school, scoffing pizza and chips in the kitchen with her son.

Will and Harry often went on double dates together away from school. Harry's social life as a young teenager was going well, although he was in danger of drifting a little when he first started secondary school. He had always assumed he would end up as some sort of entertainer when he grew up, but that ambition seemed to fade for a year or two. He still played badminton and spent time in the school gym, especially enjoying the dancing classes under the enthusiastic guidance of Miss Brocklehurst – Miss Brock to the students – but that was not a career.

Living locally was a bonus. He didn't have to stand around outside the school gates every afternoon to be assigned a seat on the bus home. This daily bussing ritual was presided over by the headmaster, Denis Oliver. He was a familiar sight, clipboard in hand and always wearing a well-used high-vis jacket. Away from his gaze, Harry and his friends would slip away across the field to the river behind the school to hang out before it was time to go home.

Harry's gang of girlfriends, who were fun, loyal and not especially serious, included Lydia Cole, Ellis Calcutt and, most importantly, Emilie Jefferies. Harry was just twelve when he first started dating Emilie but they were too young to get carried away with romance. She has remained one of his close friends from the 'old days' and she looked stunning in her ball gown on Harry's arm at their leavers' prom at the end of Year 11.

Harry has always said his first serious girlfriend was another very pretty girl at school, Abi Crawshaw, who was a key member of the school hockey team. She would go on to become head girl in the sixth form after Harry had left.

The fascinating aspect of Harry's early friendships with the opposite sex throughout his school days is that none of the girls have come forward to sell lurid tales to the tabloids. Lydia once said, 'We all love Harry to bits,' but that was all. The nearest Harry has got to revealing something juicy was to point out the place where he had his first snog. It was up against a tree down by the river. 'It was quite steamy,' was all he would say.

His dad Des recalled that he never had to sit Harry down for an excruciating 'birds and bees' conversation about sex. They would chat about things from time to time as if it were a natural part of growing up – no embarrassment.

One girl, Felicity Skinner, who wasn't from Holmes Chapel, was more forthcoming about Harry, but not in a salacious way. She said, 'He was really sweet. He was a really good boyfriend, very romantic. He was good-looking and obviously I found him very attractive.'

Felicity, who was introduced to Harry by a mutual friend in Holmes Chapel, lived in Solihull, south of Birmingham, so it was never a case of popping over to each other's houses after school. It was a long-distance teen romance that was played out mainly on the phone, although Fliss, as he called her, observed, 'It was puppy love and we were definitely each other's first love.'

Will Sweeny recalled how early on in the relationship Harry announced, 'Let's go and find her.' So they headed off to Birmingham without knowing her exact address. They knew she lived in Solihull, and that was all. 'It was pouring with rain and it took hours to find her,' Will said.

When he was with Fliss, Harry would finish work in the bakery and, instead of meeting up with his friends in Holmes Chapel, would spend his wages on a train fare south to see her. Will pointed out that she was his first very serious girlfriend: 'He really cared about her, but they were both young and it didn't work out.'

Will confirmed that Harry was not the sort of guy to play around and was not a womaniser at school. He was thoughtful where girls were concerned, and a very good listener. 'His girlfriends were long term. He was dead caring,' he said. Another close friend at school, Nick Clough, thought Harry had a precociously romantic streak where girls were concerned, a hearts and flowers boy, who preferred a candlelit dinner at his house to a can of cider by the river.

Sometimes Harry would cook a meal for his mum or run her a hot bath. She was dating Robin Twist and that was going well. They had become a settled couple, although still living in separate houses. Anne was very careful not to take her teenage children for granted and to make sure they didn't come home from school to find Robin with his feet up watching *Countdown* on TV.

Harry thought Robin was a 'really cool guy', so he was always happy to see him, sometimes texting him to come over without asking Anne first. The home in Holmes Chapel was a happy one, a tribute to his mum, who when asked about her parenting skills remarked drily, 'I make it up as I go along – like everyone else.'

On Saturdays, Harry was up before the sun, leaving the rest of the household to snooze away while he ambled down for his shift at W. Mandeville, the bakery in the centre of the village. The shop had been a fixture in Holmes Chapel since 1900, when it was founded by the great-grandfather of the present owner, Simon Wakefield. The building in Macclesfield Road even has a vintage sign on the side declaring that it is a 'Maker of HOVIS'.

There was always plenty to do before the shop opened every morning – packing orders, making sure all the shelves were correctly stocked and clearing up if any of the loaves or cakes had spilled onto the floor. Harry worked there for two and a half years, always greeting the customers with a winning smile as he stood behind the till. 'He's our boy!' said one, remembering him fondly.

At least Harry never went hungry at work. There was always some treat to try. Simon had already been baking for at least two hours before his Saturday staff arrived. His brunch pasties were especially popular as he seemed to be able to cram in a filling of bacon, sausage, scrambled egg and cheese.

Harry wasn't the only pupil from Holmes Chapel Comprehensive earning some extra cash at the bakery – there were usually three others working there too, including his close friend Nick Clough. They were teenage partners in crime, not that there was much to get up to in the village. The height of rebellion was a Chinese takeaway on a Friday night from Fortune City, which was conveniently situated two doors down from Harry's house. Harry favoured sweet and sour or crispy beef in Cantonese sauce. Then the pair of them would meet up with friends. They were too young to go to the pub so they would gather by the river and drink beer.

Nick would usually stay over at Harry's so that they could stagger bleary eyed into work together the following morning. Not many people had heard the teenage Harry sing but one memorable afternoon Nick was serving a customer when they heard Harry singing away while he was sweeping up out the back. They couldn't miss it because he hadn't realised there was anyone in the shop and was singing very loudly, as if he was in the shower at home.

'Who's singing?' asked the customer. Nick went to fetch Harry: 'I brought him out and the customer said, "Have you ever thought about singing professionally? If you ever consider it, give me a call."'

Nick knew Harry could sing because most evenings he would stroll round to the house in London Road with his guitar and practise his chords. Harry was shy about his musical ability so he usually limited himself to bashing a tambourine or singing along. By this time Harry's teenager bedroom had morphed into something out of a sitcom – cans of Lynx deodorant, clothes tossed casually onto the floor and an old Manchester United shirt pinned to the wall. His mum was fighting a losing battle shouting at him to 'TIDY UP HIS ROOM!'

Harry hadn't taken singing seriously despite both his mum and dad complimenting him when he sang in the car. Fate, however, was about to play a part when Will Sweeny decided to form a school band. He would be the drummer and he enlisted Nick to play bass and another friend, Haydn Morris, to play lead guitar. Now, they just needed a singer.

At first Harry wasn't keen. He fancied playing bass guitar, but that position was already taken. Nick recalled, 'Harry didn't think he could sing and was worried people would laugh.' The boys wouldn't take no for an answer so Harry had to get over his misgivings. Nick added, 'There was a born performer in there – he just had to find it. But when his confidence grew, he was amazing.'

The new band wanted to enter the school's Battle of the Bands competition in the summer of 2009 when Harry was fifteen. They needed a name, so Will came up with Cheese and Crackers, in honour of the legendary American band Red Hot Chili Peppers. The others gave that idea a fast thumbs down. At the time, the four of them were waiting outside a music room at school and, for reasons lost in the fog of time, the name White Eskimo popped into Will's head.

White Eskimo only had two weeks to rehearse before the big night. At least they would look the part. They all thought they were rockers or, more precisely, devotees of emo. The term standing mostly for 'emotional hardcore' embraced a punk culture that was as much about fashion as it was about music. Emo swept through the teenagers of Holmes Chapel and you couldn't pass a street corner without noticing the glint of a studded belt and a pair of tight skinny jeans, topped off with a belt made from shoelaces.

They all thought they were very cool, naturally. For once Harry was influenced by his elder sister, Gemma, although he probably loved the fashion more than the music that blared from her attic bedroom. He even let her cut his hair. She told the magazine *Another Man*, 'I had no idea what I was doing.' She did get the floppy fringe right, though, and Harry seemed pleased.

If he wasn't going to Solihull when work finished at the bakery on Saturday at 3.30 or 4pm, Harry and Nick would dash to the station a few hundred yards away to catch a train into Manchester Piccadilly. It usually took no more than three-quarters of an hour, which gave them plenty of time to hit the shops and spend their wages on a new pair of chequered trainers.

One of the fashion statements associated with the emo culture was a piercing. Nick suggested that they had their ears pierced one afternoon when they were in Manchester. Harry wasn't keen, concerned that his mum might not approve. He didn't even have a discreet tattoo until he was eighteen.

For the big evening at Holmes Chapel, Harry looked the part, choosing to wear a plain white shirt and black tie – more Robert Palmer than My Chemical Romance. They were very accomplished for an inexperienced school band, performing just two songs: 'Summer of '69' by Bryan Adams and the evergreen 'Are You Gonna Be My Girl' by Jet, which was much rockier. The audience was very enthusiastic, with a host of schoolgirls gathering at the front. White Eskimo won, pocketing £100 in cash and getting the chance to perform at the local arts festival, Goosfest, based in the nearby village of Goostry.

In those very early days, Harry was already a natural front-man, even if he sang in a slightly strained manner with his neck strangling the sound, suggesting he could benefit from some vocal coaching. Harry is modest about his time with White Eskimo but they were popular locally, playing an eclectic mix of songs. At a White Eskimo concert you might hear The Beatles classic 'A Hard Day's Night', 'Valerie' by the Zutons – later made famous by Amy Whitehouse and Mark Ronson – 'First Date' by American rock band Blink-182 and Paolo Nutini's 'Jenny Don't Be Hasty'; and one they wrote themselves, 'Gone in a Week'.

The most they made from a gig was for the wedding party of the mother of one the girls from school. They had to learn a couple of extra Bob Marley songs that were the bride's favourites, but they were paid a handsome £400 for the occasion.

At school, GCSEs were looming and Harry was looking to the future, planning what he would study in the sixth form. Although he might not match the academic prowess of Gemma, he would have little trouble passing his exams and looking to continue with career-orientated subjects including law, business and sociology.

His mum, however, had other ideas for her son.

3

LOVELY NEWS

———

Harry asked Simon Wakefield for the day off. He wasn't just working Saturdays now, he was swinging by the bakery after school during the week to spend an hour or two helping to clear and clean to earn some extra cash. His GCSEs were imminent and, if they went well, he intended to go on to college for further studies. He wasn't sure exactly what career he wanted to pursue but there was talk of becoming a physio-therapist somewhere down the line. It was a career Abi was keen on, so they had talked about the possibility and Harry thought it seemed promising if the rock-star plan didn't bear fruit.

Simon readily agreed when Harry told him he was going for an audition for *The X Factor*. Harry had been feeling a bit unsettled since Gemma had left home to go to Sheffield Hallam University, where she was studying Science Education with a qualified teacher status. She was just as academically brilliant as she had always been. She observed, 'It was only after I had left home that I realised he would actually miss me.'

He couldn't ask the school's permission to miss classes for a TV audition, so he took the traditional solution – he skived off. Will Sweeny went with him on the day to offer moral support.

White Eskimo were still very much a band but perhaps it was time for Harry to strike out on his own. He's never properly explained why he decided to go it alone, but a casual look at the show's history (this would be the seventh series) revealed that groups had never won and, apart from JLS, hadn't done particularly well afterwards. Bands playing instruments were definitely nowhere to be seen.

In the finest traditions of mums, Anne encouraged him to fill out the application form. In the end, she did it for him and sent it off. He was given a date at the end of April 2010, along with literally thousands of others, to roll up to Old Trafford to meet the advance production staff. These were the unheralded judges who would decide who was going to go through to the next stage. It was never just a case of being able to sing well; contestants had to be good TV, so being quirky, amusing or possessing a twinkle were qualities as important as hitting the right notes.

The audition was bedlam, with more than 6,000 hopefuls jamming the car park, all wanting to be chosen. They had come from right across the north of England to queue up for literally hours, just hoping to be noticed. Will and Harry hung around for four or five hours. Like everyone else, Harry had to wait to hear if he had won through to the first televised audition stage when he would have to sing in front of the judges. It was good news.

Simon Cowell and co. were not there at this first stage but host Dermot O'Leary was on duty to give the crowd a rousing pep talk. The *Manchester Evening News* also sent along a reporter and photographer. They didn't see Harry but they did spot Emma Chawner, who seemed to enter every year, as well as a young woman from Liverpool who had failed to make the televised stages four years earlier. However, this time, Rebecca Ferguson, a twenty-three-year-old mother-of-two, sang 'River Deep Mountain High' and sailed through.

When Harry heard that he would be at the first televised audition in Manchester, he was sent a list of possible songs and told that he needed to choose and prepare two for the big day. He went for the Stevie Wonder standard 'Isn't She Lovely' with the back-up of 'Hey, Soul Sister', which had been a hit the previous year for the American rock band Train. Nobody knew it then but the latter was much more in keeping with the artist that Harry Styles would become.

For the moment, 'Isn't She Lovely' was the front runner. The classic was older than Harry. Stevie Wonder had written it for his *Songs in the Key of Life*, one of the great albums of the seventies. The lyrics refer to the birth of his daughter, Aisha, and might be regarded as either sweet or cheesy depending on one's taste. The song was quite a daring choice for a sixteen-year-old boy, because the performance could easily become corny if Harry overdid the saccharine and the smile.

He needed to practise, but to his mum and sister's surprise, he seemed quite shy when it came to rehearsing. The boy who had a karaoke machine in his bedroom and already sang in a group at school was suddenly bashful. He made sure the bathroom door was firmly shut as he wailed, 'Isn't she won … dur … ful.' He had no idea the two women were sat on the landing outside, excitedly listening to every note.

The reason for Harry's new-found reticence is simply explained. When he was part of White Eskimo he could be Bryan Adams singing 'Summer of '69' or John Mayer performing 'Free Fallin''. In his bedroom, enjoying karaoke, he was Bowie, Jagger or Elvis. In front of the *X Factor* judges, though, there would be no hiding place: he needed to be Harry Styles from Holmes Chapel and show them he had what it took to be a star.

This was the golden age of *The X Factor*, a top-rated show that made stars not just for lucky finalists but also for the judges, who up until now were more famous than the artists they discovered. Some of the winners, including Alexandra Burke, Joe McElderry and, especially, Leona Lewis, had become household names, but they were all eclipsed by Simon Cowell.

Simon may not have spent his Saturdays in a bakery, but he left school at sixteen and was a tea boy, a runner and then worked in the post room at EMI before edging his way up the record-business ladder. He had been a senior A&R consultant responsible for the cringeworthy Robson & Jerome hits before *Pop Idol* began in 2001. He had brokered an agreement whereby the winner would release their first record on his label, S Records, and, keen to protect his investment, he was persuaded to become a judge – a role, it soon became apparent, he was born to play. His famous clash with eventual winner Will Young was television gold.

By the end of the first series, Simon was on his way to becoming a television institution. He was not especially witty or clever in addressing the hopefuls but he had a style and method that was essential viewing on a Saturday night. We expect Simon Cowell to be rude and are genuinely pleased when he is.

After a couple of series of *Pop Idol*, Simon was able to introduce his own series, *The X Factor*, to British TV. A complicated legal case involving the mastermind behind *Pop Idol*, the former Spice Girls' manager Simon Fuller, ended with a financial settlement that allowed Cowell to pursue *The X Factor* in the UK while working for Fuller in the US on *American Idol*. Together, these shows propelled Simon Cowell into superstar status on both sides of the Atlantic.

Behind the scenes, Simon was known as The Dark Lord, but in reality he is one of the most charming men in the business. The radio host and former television critic Kevin O'Sullivan observed, 'He is great company and he kind of loves you, that's his charm. You are sucked in.'

Simon is, however, primarily a businessman not a TV personality. Behind the scenes in 2010 he had formed the Syco Entertainment Group, a joint venture with Sony Music that gave him enormous fire power for cross-promoting between television and records. Having this power behind you almost guaranteed success for the acts he wanted to promote.

He understood, though, that he needed to keep *The X Factor* fresh in order to maintain its success. He had, for instance, introduced an audience for the televised auditions and so Harry, in 2010, faced that additional pressure.

But he was not a clairvoyant, and he could not have foreseen the path that Harry Styles would take when he was confronted by the sixteen-year-old boy from Holmes Chapel at the Manchester Central Hall, on the site of the city's old railway station.

Harry had dressed very carefully for the occasion. He chose a plain white t-shirt, a light-grey cardigan and a slightly darker-grey, patterned scarf hanging loosely in casual bohemian style around his neck. 'The outfit spoke volumes,' observed fashion commentator Alison Jane Reid. 'Harry is clearly interested in fashion and in making a statement. A scarf is a good place to start. It shows individuality from the moment he stepped into the public gaze. Few men would choose to accessorise a classic white t-shirt with a scarf, which he has chosen to wear in an artful, interesting way. It hints at what is to come.'

Harry radiated good health, but that had not been the case the previous day: he couldn't stop throwing up. When he started coughing up blood as well, it was time for a trip to the local hospital in Northwich. There didn't seem to be an explanation, so perhaps it was an acute case of old-fashioned nerves. He gradually felt calm enough to go ahead and on the day itself there was no outward sign of any apprehension.

Team Styles was there to support him, including Mum, Gemma and Robin Twist, who was now a welcome family fixture and much appreciated by Harry. To begin his day, Harry and his crew had to speak to Dermot O'Leary, who pretended he had just stumbled across them in a crowd of people.

Harry stood out but his 'team' were distinctive as well, wearing t-shirts that declared 'We Think Harry Has the X Factor'. He told Dermot, 'I'm Harry Styles. I'm sixteen and I'm from Holmes Chapel in Cheshire. It's a bit boring. Nothing much happens. It's picturesque.'

He revealed that he was in a band with school friends called White Eskimo, which was a great plug for the group, and mentioned their Battle of the Bands triumph. He also explained the experience of that competition had prompted his singing ambitions: 'I got such a thrill when I was in front of people singing that it made me want to do it more and more.'

Harry seemed a natural in front of the camera, cracking a joke: 'People tell me I can sing – it's usually my mother.' Dermot, laughing, added, 'They always say that.'

Anne gave her son a kiss and a hug before he went on stage to meet the judges and face a young crowd of some 3,000 *X Factor* fans. Harry was still a teenage boy but there was no sign of embarrassment about receiving a kiss from his mum … in public!

The judges panel for that year was Simon Cowell, Cheryl Cole, Dannii Minogue and, old favourite, Louis Walsh, but there were some early problems. Dannii had missed all the auditions around the country because of her first pregnancy and had given birth to her son Ethan earlier in the month. Cheryl Cole, as she was then, was arguably the most famous woman in the country that year – and certainly the most photographed. While Harry caught the train into Manchester for his first *X Factor* experience, Cheryl was named the World's Sexiest Woman by *FHM* for the second year running. The magazine said, 'No one was even on the same continent in terms of votes.'

The following month she was headline news when she filed for divorce against footballer Ashley Cole, citing his unreasonable behaviour as the grounds. In July, just before she was due to judge Harry's first performance in front of the television cameras, she returned from a break in Tanzania with a dose of malaria that meant she needed complete rest and would not be on the panel in Manchester.

Her stand-in was the Pussycat Dolls singer Nicole Scherzinger, then just starting out on British television. She was a natural, though, and would prove to be very popular, taking on the role of a permanent judge in subsequent years. To begin with she needed to give her opinion on Harry.

He hadn't seemed at all nervous when he told Simon that he was planning to go to college. He sang a soupçon of 'Isn't She Lovely' a cappella and was robustly in tune. He finished and did a little bow to the audience. Nicole was impressed, saying, 'You could really hear how great your voice was.'

On this occasion, Louis Walsh was the Grinch. He thought Harry was too young, which prompted Simon to play the good cop and encourage the audience to boo his fellow panellist. Even Harry gave a boo to Louis when he decided that it was a 'no from me'. At least the famed boyband manager didn't come out with one of his well-worn clichés: 'You remind me of a young Cliff Richard.'

Simon did suggest that Harry might benefit from some vocal coaching – perhaps reflecting that Harry was trying a little too hard. 'You actually could be very good,' said Simon. He cast his deciding vote in Harry's favour. The outcome never really seemed in doubt, but Harry didn't know that and described it as 'one of the best moments of my life'.

The problem now was not being able to shout his progress from the rooftops of Holmes Chapel. His support team were all sworn to secrecy and Harry went back to working in the bakery, knowing that in a couple of months' time he would be on his way to London for the Bootcamp stage.

As before, he asked Simon Wakefield for the day off. But this time, he didn't go back.

4

A SECOND CHANCE

Gemma drove Harry down to Wembley Arena for the start of Bootcamp and left him when she saw he was in his element chatting and laughing with the other contenders still living the dream in the car park – so far so good. Clearly, it was just going to be a nice day out. That was before Simon Cowell addressed everyone.

The first day of Bootcamp is the most brutal. Simon told the hopefuls: 'Today, you're going to be put into your categories and you're going to sing one song. There are literally no second chances today.' The Boys had to perform 'Man in the Mirror' from Michael Jackson's 1987 album *Bad*. The song had been re-released in 2009 following Jackson's death and had reached number two in the charts – so for many it was very much a modern track.

It's a serious song that's wasted on a lot of young men hoping to progress on a Saturday night variety show. 'Man in the Mirror' is a call for change; the need for all of us to look at ourselves in tackling prejudice and discrimination. Jackson's video had featured images of starving black children in Africa, the homeless, and important figures from our immediate past including Dr Martin Luther King Jr., President Nelson Mandela and Archbishop Desmond Tutu – cut powerfully against images of the Ku Klux Klan and Hitler. It wasn't subtle, but it was more effective because of that. One can only imagine the images that would be included if the song were re-released today, in the wake of George Floyd's murder.

The song's message was the least of Harry's worries on this warm July day in north-west London. Michael Jackson songs are very hard to sing but he did a passable version and was invited back the following day. More than 200 contestants had already been trimmed by half.

That evening he enjoyed celebrating with other contenders at the hotel in Wembley where they were all housed during Bootcamp. Reports suggested that Harry had a few drinks before heading off for an early night. They didn't suggest that he might not have been alone, although later it was revealed he enjoyed a Bootcamp fling with a young blonde singer from Stroud in Gloucestershire called Katie Smith.

Next morning, it was dancing day, which always makes for good television as those hapless contestants with two left feet do their best Fred Astaire impression. Some of them are born dad dancers. Harry, however, was a natural. He may not have been ready to join Diversity, the inspiring street-dance troupe who had won *Britain's Got Talent* in 2009, but he had rhythm.

Harry didn't broadcast it but he loved dancing at school. That was not the case for Zayn Malik, a seventeen-year-old from Bradford, though. It may or may not have been a set-up but he refused to join the other boys on stage, claiming to camera, 'I hate dancing.'

Zayn had form when it came to being the reluctant pop star. He had to be pushed out of the door by his mum Trisha to go to his judges' audition: 'He chickened out, saying, "Can't I just leave it?"' She had to softly persuade him that he had nothing to lose and he should just see what happened.

Trisha had converted to Islam when she married Yasser Malik and they settled into a rented terrace house in the East Bowling district of the city. She made sure Zayn and his three sisters read the Koran and attended the local mosque. She worked as a halal chef in the kitchen of a primary school, where she prepared meals for the Muslim children.

Zayn had three yeses from the judges in Manchester, one better than Harry, for singing the smooth, Grammy Award-winning hit 'Let Me Love You' by Mario. The song perfectly suited his crystal-clear, soulful voice. While he was obviously very good-looking, Zayn seemed to lack Harry's twinkly charisma – and that was before he 'felt like an idiot' when the dancing began.

Simon Cowell personally had to go and find him backstage, sitting by himself. Simon persuaded him to continue, telling him 'the only person he was hurting was himself'. It was great TV. Zayn clearly wasn't as good a mover as Harry but he wasn't totally useless either, and the episode made sure he was noticed.

Harry, dressed in his favourite purple hoodie, danced immediately behind Zayn so we noticed him as well. The choreographer in charge of the day was, as usual, Brian Friedman, and he later observed, 'Zayn was better than he thought.' He was also in no doubt about a seldom-publicised fact about the boys who would eventually form One Direction: 'Harry was definitely the best dancer.'

Having navigated his way through the dancing, Harry had to choose a song from a list of forty to perform for the panel the following day when the final six for Judges' Houses would be chosen. He went with 'Stop Crying Your Heart Out', a top-ten hit for Oasis in 2002. The Noel Gallagher-written song had enjoyed a revival when Leona Lewis recorded it in 2009.

Unsurprisingly, her version was on the Syco label, so giving it a free plug on his TV show demonstrated once more Simon Cowell's astute commercial awareness: never miss an opportunity to make money. The Oasis version featured Liam Gallagher's unique vocal style, while Leona gave it a touch more emotion. Undoubtedly it's a beautiful song, but it was too mature for a sixteen-year-old boy. Harry had picked it because it was one he could perform without fear of making a mistake. 'My performance was so boring,' he said, truthfully. He also drew the short straw of being first on among the boys. Another hopeful, Liam Payne from Wolverhampton, also sang it – unmemorably.

Decision time had arrived. Simon read out the final list of boys chosen to go to Judges' Houses. Cranking up the tension, just two spots remained and Harry had still not been picked. The next successful candidate was Matt Cardle, a singer from Essex. Matt was twenty-seven, so in previous years would not have been eligible for the Boys' category, but in 2010 the producers changed the goalposts and made the age limit twenty-eight. Apparently it was Nicole Scherzinger's idea but it made good commercial sense. If Matt happened to win the competition, he would appeal immediately to a younger audience than if he was stuck in the older category.

At this point, Matt's good fortune was Harry's loss. The final choice was a sixteen-year-old from South Wales called Tom Richards. Five young men in particular, including a tearful Harry, were left heartbroken … but it was the best thing that ever happened to them.

Harry was sitting disconsolately on his suitcase in the car park of Wembley Arena. He was chatting to another contestant, Niall Horan, who had travelled over from County Westmeath in the Republic of Ireland and had just had the same crushing disappointment. Niall had been one of the most popular among the other contestants at Bootcamp, always strumming away on his guitar and leading a group sing.

Niall had been a natural entertainer as a youngster, playing the title role in the musical *Oliver* at school, teaching himself guitar by watching YouTube videos, singing in the back of the car and being told by relations that he would be famous one day. Like Harry, his parents had split when he was very young and he had grown up dividing his time between the two of them.

Before his audition he had explained that he had been compared a few times to Justin Bieber. He was a cute sixteen-year-old, which was definitely not how he wanted to be viewed, but the judges, in particular fellow Irishman Louis Walsh, thought he had the likeability factor after he sang 'So Sick' by singer-songwriter Ne-Yo, who, in the small world of music, had also written Zayn's audition song 'Let Me Love You'. Simon brought Niall down to earth by observing, 'You are not as good as you thought you were,' before giving him a yes. Guest judge Katy Perry noted that 'likeableness is not going to sell records,' which was almost certainly not true.

Niall had also been sunk at Bootcamp by a weak version of an Oasis song – in his case, 'Champagne Supernova' – before joining Harry as a reject. Both boys really had no idea that they were not finished after all. The groups were not that strong in 2010, so behind the scenes it was decided to place some of the boys and girls who had nearly made it into two new bands. Simon Cowell explained the reasoning: 'The groups that year were actually pretty bad.'

Both Nicole Scherzinger and Simon Cowell have claimed the credit for suggesting a boy band of also-rans. It was Simon. He explained to *Rolling Stone* magazine that he was relying on his gut instinct, taking just fifteen minutes to decide which five boys he was going to bring back as a group.

They were Niall, Zayn, Liam Payne, Louis Tomlinson from Doncaster and Harry. They were called back on stage but they genuinely had no idea why. Simon gave Nicole the task of telling them that they weren't out of the competition after all.

As ever, it was classic *X Factor* television, especially when Harry sank to his knees in delight at the news that they would be going to Judges' Houses when the series returned in September The boys all jumped around and hugged each other – lottery winners in life.

Simon told them to take five minutes to think about it and what this news meant for their futures. They needed five seconds, although Liam, who had invested so much time and energy on being a singer, probably needed a little longer.

The major surprise was not that Harry was chosen for the group but that he had not been picked as a solo artist for the

Boys' section in the first place. Simon was once asked how he could *not* put through someone with such obvious charm and presence, not to mention talent, as a solo act. He admitted that the biggest single factor was his age. Harry was a sixteen-year-old boy from Holmes Chapel who might have been lost if he had gone up against Matt Cardle, ten years older and a seasoned professional.

From the very beginning, at the first audition, Simon had seen something in Harry, declaring enthusiastically: 'This kid's got everything: he's really confident, he's got unbelievable charisma, and he's a good singer. He wasn't a great singer on his first audition, but he was a *good* singer and everyone gravitated towards him. He was exactly what you're looking for when you make one of these shows: memorable and a natural frontman.'

He almost revealed too much. Simon had been around long enough to understand stardom. Kevin O'Sullivan confirmed, 'Cowell does have a serious talent for spotting what the masses will love.' All five boys had an edge, a talent that added to the collective but Harry was the one who, in his words, had 'unbelievable charisma' and was a 'natural frontman'. Simon is far too shrewd to admit it openly but it's easy to conclude that the boy band was actually formed *around* Harry Styles.

Manufacturing a boy band or girl band was nothing new, so this wasn't a 'eureka' moment patented by *The X Factor*. In the nineties, both Take That and the Spice Girls were put together by forward-thinking managers. Robbie Williams' entire career began when he spotted an advertisement in a local paper that stated simply, 'Singers and dancers wanted for a new boy band.'

The Spice Girls followed the same formula – although this time the ad was in *The Stage* in amongst the jobs for dancers in Dubai and cruise ship cabaret entertainers. If members of both these iconic groups had been ten years older then it's a racing certainty they would have been trying to impress Simon Cowell.

He himself had form when it came to manufacturing a boy band. Back in the late nineties, he had joined forces with Chris Herbert, the man who put together the Spice Girls, to find a boy band. This time the ad placed in *The Stage* said, 'Spice Boys Wanted'. They were put up in a house in Camberley, Surrey, to see if they gelled as a unit and to prepare.

They were called 5ive, and, before disbanding in 2001, had achieved a dozen top ten hits, including topping the album charts. They sold ten million records worldwide and, perhaps just as significantly, were on twenty-three magazine covers and secured some lucrative commercial deals, including a link-up with Pepsi.

They were a useful template for Simon Cowell's next boy-band venture, although Chris Herbert's philosophy for 5ive was perhaps not right for good-looking teenage boys on Saturday night prime-time TV. He explained what he was looking for with 5ive: 'Take That would give you roses but I wanted a band that would fuck you up against a garage door.'

What was needed was something in between – a blend of romance and naughtiness – that Simon thought he had found in the cheeky yet winning smile of Harry Styles.

When 5ive disbanded in 2001, television was about to transform the search for fame. Now, stardom could be grasped instantly and the gradual progress of Take That, the Spice Girls and 5ive was, for the moment at least, a thing of the past. The show *Popstars* in 2001 was the game changer. Talent shows, it seemed, hadn't much evolved since the 'good old days' of *Opportunity Knocks* and *New Faces*. But now, after just six weeks, three girls and two boys were chosen by a panel of judges to be the members of a new British band called Hear'Say.

The power of TV was seldom so well illustrated as when their easy-listening single 'Pure and Simple' became the fast-est-selling debut record of all time. The attraction of a reality pop show was clear – big ratings and a guaranteed number one hit record with something inoffensive and middle of the road.

The short-lived career of Hear'Say revealed some flaws in the idea. First, you can't have much of a future if the group don't have a connection. Secondly, a mix of boys and girls thins the fan base rather than expands it: far better to have one or the other. When the all-male Take That first disbanded in the nineties, it was the all-female Spice Girls who slipped into the empty chair.

These lessons were soon learned. When the next 'discover a new band' series, *Popstars: The Rivals*, was broadcast in autumn 2002, it was promoted as a rivalry between a boy band and a girl band. The idea was clever and commercially astute – auditions, Bootcamp, judges' visits and live shows would create excitement throughout the series, which ended with the final group of boys going up against the girls to see who would have the Christmas number one.

Looking back, one could be forgiven for not even remem-bering the name of the winning boy band. They were called

One True Voice, a cheesy name, and fittingly they recorded a saccharine-heavy version of a Bee Gees' song, 'Sacred Trust'. The girls, on the other hand, became Girls Aloud and their single 'Sound of the Underground' was an instant classic. The renowned music critic Alexis Petridis observed, 'It was a reality pop record that didn't make you want to do physical harm to everyone involved in its manufacture.'

Surprisingly, the bookies initially had One True Voice as favourites to be the seasonal number one, but it soon became clear that Girls Aloud would win and step into the shoes recently vacated by the Spice Girls. One True Voice split up within a year, perhaps hinting that there wasn't room for two *Popstars'* bands.

By the time Simon Cowell was putting together an *X Factor* boy band in 2010, Girls Aloud had achieved twenty-one hit singles and Cheryl was on her way to becoming the most successful female solo artist in the UK.

But, just as One True Voice are all but forgotten, so are the all-girl group of also-rans that Simon picked at the same time as the boys who would form One Direction. At this early stage, Belle Amie, as they would become, had every chance of being *the* winning combination. The public would soon have the chance to make known their preference. The four girls were just as surprised to be selected and as enthusiastic as the boys.

The next significant event for the boys was discovering which judge would be their mentor. Simon was handed the groups – again, a fortunate break for the five. They might have stood a better chance of winning with Cheryl or Dannii, but Simon's influence was far-reaching and global, something that would be of huge benefit to Harry's future. It was no coincidence that Simon had been the mentor of Leona Lewis, the biggest act to date to come out of the UK *X Factor*.

The first consideration for the as-yet-unnamed boy band was a discussion about what they were going to wear. Louis Tomlinson, as always, looked immaculate, so they could just copy what he was wearing. Harry needed to ditch the beanie that seemed to be glued to his head. Then they had to measure each other's heights to make sure they would all fit nicely into team photographs and wouldn't have one person disappearing out of shot.

More importantly, they needed to properly get to know one another. Louis was the oldest at eighteen and Harry, at sixteen, was the youngest, so there wasn't a huge age difference. These two teenage boys had got on well from the outset but now the *X Factor* team needed to see if there was any chemistry between all five.

They hit upon the unoriginal plan of the five of them staying together in a house for a week – a chance to bond and to create some footage for when they went to Judges' Houses. Harry told *The X Factor* that his mum's partner, Robin, had a bungalow in the grounds of his house near Congleton. He could check but they could probably have the place to themselves.

The *X Factor* producers liked this idea, so a week or so before Judges' Houses, four teenage boys arrived in Cheshire to see if they would get on. Zayn was the last to arrive, perhaps already a hint that he would be the one to find it the most difficult to blend with the others.

Harry was ready to show them around his home patch. It was like freshers' week at university – slobbing out and making friends before proper work began. Anne and Robin sensibly left the teenage boys to get on with it. The accommodation was a step up from student digs, especially because they had the use of a swimming pool in the garden, which also doubled as a 'jumpers for goalposts' football pitch. Anne popped some sensible food in the fridge but this was ignored in favour of Super Noodles and supplies from the nearest KFC.

The most important aspect of the week was that the boys got to know one another – they were just lads having a laugh. Harry, in particular, had an instant rapport with Louis Tomlinson, who was even more boisterous than him and could break any tension in the room with a jokey remark. He was also the best at football and a lifelong supporter of his hometown team, Doncaster Rovers.

Like Harry, he had been brought up primarily by his mother, Johannah, who split from his father when Louis was just two. He was estranged from his dad throughout his child-hood and took the name Tomlinson from her second marriage.

Despite his obvious good looks, Louis wasn't the brooding teenage heartthrob at school, preferring instead to be the class clown. His teenage journey was remarkably similar to Harry's, initially gaining a love of performing through drama and he too was in a school band, playing songs by Oasis and Green Day and generally being more rock-oriented than White Eskimo.

Initially, it looked as if acting might be the way forward for him. His younger twin half-sisters, Phoebe and Daisy, were in demand for roles at a very young age and he would accompany them to various sets, acting as big brother chap-erone for the day and earning £30 for sitting around.

41

Occasionally he would be roped in as an extra, which he found 'super-exciting'.

He was only eleven when he was given one line to say in *Fat Friends*, an ITV drama about a weekly slimming club. Among others, it starred James Corden, who would become one of Harry's best friends in showbusiness. Phoebe and Daisy were cast as babies.

He joined a drama society in Barnsley when he was at Hall Cross school, but could only go when his mum, who everyone called Jay, could afford the fees. He appeared occasionally on television; in 2006, aged fourteen, he was uncredited in the one-off crime drama *If I Had You*, which starred Sarah Parish and Paul McGann. Louis was one of four boys who found a dead body floating in a lake.

More relevantly for his future career, he starred in a production of *Grease* at Hall Cross, dressed all in black in the John Travolta role of Danny Zuko. A high-school musical was probably the best training for being in a boy band and helped to engender a love of performing in the teenage Louis.

He auditioned for *The X Factor* in 2009 but didn't make it past the first producer's assessment. Undaunted, he had another go the following year and offered something extra to the new group, even if he was arguably the weakest singer. After performing 'Hey There Delilah' by Plain White T's at his live audition he said simply, 'I sang terribly.'

The one potential hurdle for the new band was that Louis and Liam did not get on. They had very different personalities. Louis was bumptious and Liam was more serious, aware that this was his big chance – the others would joke that he was the dad of the band. He acknowledged, 'I was a bit too grown up. I needed to grow down.' He also didn't have any crazy mates – all his friends were quiet, so being with a group of rowdy boys was a jolt.

Liam nearly had a career as an athlete. He was a member of his local Wolverhampton and Bilston Athletic Club and, as a boy, would run five miles before school. He might have ditched performing altogether if he had been selected for the England national schools' team.

That disappointment encouraged him to move from karaoke to stage productions and he joined a local theatre group for which he dressed all in white to play the John Travolta starring role of Tony Romero in *Saturday Night Fever*. His career was already the most advanced of the newly formed boy band – he had sung in front of the crowd at Molyneux before a Wolves' home game against Manchester United.

Liam had also come close to progressing in a previous *X Factor* series, and he was determined not to squander the opportunity this time round. In 2008 he made it to Judges' Houses in Barbados, having just turned fifteen. He wasn't chosen for the Live Shows, but Simon had suggested he try again in two years' time.

Liam was installed as one of the favourites for the whole competition after his 2010 audition when he sang the Michael Bublé version of the old standard 'Cry Me a River' and Simon had stood up to applaud. But, like Harry, he should have steered well clear of a Liam Gallagher song at Bootcamp.

The problem going forward for the new band was that both Louis and Liam wanted to be its leader. The two came to an unwritten understanding that they would keep that animosity within the group and not let on to potential fans or Simon.

Liam, however, revealed, 'We absolutely hated each other. It was so funny. Really bad. We hid it well.'

At least the lads were all keen on sport – Liam was talented at running and boxing; Zayn, too, was a decent boxer; Louis was the man for football; Niall was pretty good at football but golf was his game. Harry would have had no competition from the others on the badminton court.

Aside from the high spirits of a free holiday, the new band needed to rehearse for their trip to Judges' Houses and that presented yet another problem: how to decide who would sing each part. That 'cut-throat decision' was too difficult at this early stage and so, to start with, they sang each number in unison. 'It was a horrible thing,' said Liam.

They managed to come up with a name they all liked. Harry suggested One Direction because they were all heading in one direction. Someone else came up with USP and another idea was Status Single. Fortunately these alternatives were quickly put in the bin and One Direction was born. It just stuck, so if nothing else came of it, at least they had a good name.

The reality had yet to sink in that at some point soon they would have to impress Simon Cowell – that would be make or break.

5

TORN

They hadn't actually performed one song together but the newly named One Direction were swanning around by yet another swimming pool, this time in the sun-drenched resort of Marbella, in Southern Spain. For the moment, *The X Factor* seemed to be nothing more than a summer camp.

Even Liam and Louis were putting on a united front, realising the opportunity they had been given depended on them being 'all for one, one for all'. In the short term, they were told by the producers to prepare an acoustic version of 'Torn', one of the biggest hits of the nineties. Originally the song was written and recorded by the Californian rock band Ednaswap, but it became a million-seller after it was released as a single in 1997 by former *Neighbours* star Natalie Imbruglia.

The general public were used to 'Torn' being sung by a female singer, so it would offer something different to hear it performed by a boy band. The rehearsals hadn't gone smoothly because Louis had been stung by a sea urchin when they were splashing around by the beach, so he was in casualty while the other four practised in the villa grounds.

Louis was trying not to grimace with pain when, nursing a red and swollen foot, he joined the others to sing in front of Simon and his usual guest judge, Sinitta, who was looking fabulous. Louis was hardly needed because, in effect, it was the Harry show, as the 'natural frontman'.

Liam sang two verses before Harry, wearing the same lucky audition white t-shirt and scarf, took over for the rest of the song, with some background oohs from the others and a sweet harmony from Zayn. Afterwards Simon said, 'See you later,' and had a chat with Sinitta. They agreed the boys were cool, although Simon thought they were a 'little bit timid'.

That was just for the television filming. In reality, he was already seeing the pound signs where One Direction was concerned. As soon as the cameras were switched off, he sprang up and declared, 'These guys are incredible!' In reality, he had taken 'one-millionth' of a second to realise that this was the group he would be backing – and not just for the next week or two.

Back on television he cranked up the tension by declaring that it was a tough choice: 'My head is saying it's a risk and my heart is saying you deserve a shot.' It was no surprise whatsoever when he concluded, 'Guys, I've gone with my heart – you're through!'

Once more there was a gap between Judges' Houses and the beginning of the live finals, when it was practically impossible for Harry to conceal his excitement. He stopped using Facebook, kept a low profile in Holmes Chapel and ventured out just to go to Manchester to shop for clothes. He had to borrow some money from his mum to brighten up his wardrobe for what he hoped would be a much longer stay in London.

He opted for his favourite well-known brands, including Topman, Hollister and Jack Wills, responsible for his much-worn purple hoodie. Alison Jane Reid was unimpressed: 'I wouldn't call the purple Jack Wills hoodie stylish. It screams, "I am a Jack Wills hoodie!" It's loud. It's the logo uniform of teenagers obsessed with consumerist status symbols. The most interesting thing is that Harry chose to wear it in purple. That's daring. It shows already his love of experimentation with fashion and desire to stand out through the choices he makes.'

At sixteen, Harry was yet to be inducted into the fashion world, but there was already an adventurous edge to what he chose to wear. That was evident when he paraded around the latest *X Factor* house wearing nothing but a gold leopard-print thong that a friend had given him for his birthday back in Holmes Chapel.

Apparently, Harry would have considered the thong being overdressed, often lounging around the house naked if he felt like it. He explained, 'Stripping off is very liberating. I feel free. It's always a spur of the moment thing, but no one seemed to mind.'

Perhaps Harry was fortunate that nobody cared. Ten years on and it would only take one complaint for his stock to fall rapidly – from cheeky, mischievous chap to weird perv who would flash his bits in front of the telly. The actor John Barrowman was axed in 2021 as a judge on *Dancing on Ice* when allegations surfaced of him flashing numerous times on the set of *Doctor Who* and *Torchwood*. He called it 'tomfoolery'.

That excuse doesn't wear so well when you are a middle-aged man, but it's ok to be high-spirited at sixteen.

Fortunately for Harry, everyone realised he was just a scamp of a teenager having a laugh. He volunteered, 'I think Mary secretly liked it.'

The Mary in question was the Irish singer Mary Byrne, the Tesco check-out cashier who made it to *The X Factor* finals at the age of fifty. She and Harry became great friends and she really didn't mind her daily eyeful. She recalled, 'Every morning One Direction would come into the studio where we rehearsed and they always gave me a kiss. But Harry went further, he'd moon at me, the cheeky little boy! And it wasn't as if I wanted to see his bottom – it's just like a baby's bottom.'

The studio Mary mentions was a large room in the house that was given over to musical practice. The boys spent most of their time in the 'bean bag' room, their name for the relaxation area, the common room of the house where they could play table tennis or Nintendo Wii.

So far, the *X Factor* experience seemed to be moving from one slice of five-star accommodation to the next. The 2010 mansion was a stunning Spanish-style villa with seven bedrooms close to Borehamwood, just north of London. The previous year had been a nightmare for neighbours when the house between Hampstead and Golders Green was mobbed daily by excited fans of the show and its contestants.

The teenage boys of One Direction did not seem to appreciate their luxurious surroundings, complaining that they had to share the smallest room. The producers gave them a list of rules, which they promptly put in the bin. The first was to keep their room tidy, which was never going to happen with five teenage lads. If you lifted up a t-shirt casually scrunched up and thrown onto the floor, you were more than likely to find the remains of the previous night's takeaway. Nobody bothered making a bed.

The former *Blue Peter* host Konnie Huq, who this year had taken over from Holly Willoughby to present the companion show *The Xtra Factor*, described it simply as a 'pigsty'. The girls from Belle Amie, who had also made it through to the Live Finals, gamely tried to tidy it a little but had to give up. At least they didn't have to share a bathroom with the boys. That room was almost as bad and made public conveniences seem like four-star luxury. Liam, in particular, said he found it hard sharing with the others, especially as his old enemy Louis was the messiest.

The biggest drawback regarding the room, however, was Harry's snoring; the others would complain and tell him to shut up – with little success.

The theme of the first live show at the Fountain Studios, Wembley, in October 2010 was Number Ones. The producers in consultation with Simon handed One Direction the multiple Grammy Award-winning 'Viva la Vida', the 2008 classic from Coldplay. The track is not a simplistic Spanish holiday song – 'Long Live Life' – but a title inspired by the great Mexican painter Frida Kahlo.

Her 1954 work 'Viva la Vida' was her last painting before her death that year, aged forty-seven. It depicts watermelons in various shapes and shades of green, symbolising perhaps the passing of time in one's life. Frida had spent a lifetime dealing with chronic physical pain – a result of childhood polio and a crippling bus accident at the age of eighteen. She was in rapidly declining health after having a leg amputated. She scrawled 'Viva la vida' on the flesh of one of the melons.

The significance of the painting was not lost on the accomplished songwriters of Coldplay, a group that had long been one of Harry's favourites. They used it as a starting point for their own reflections on the passage of time and the ending of life. From the point of view of lyrics, it's not an easy song to learn. There are just so many lines.

One Direction knuckled down under the guidance of Texas-born vocal producer Savan Kotecha, who would play a leading role in their musical development, especially as a songwriter. They were the second group on and Harry had little to do this time, other than sing the chorus and thrust his shoulder provocatively at the audience, for some reason.

Most importantly, and this was true of any week, they needed to stay in the competition. They were never going to win. Within a couple of weeks, it was clear that Matt Cardle was miles ahead. He was always a commanding favourite with the bookies and would come first in eleven out of twelve public votes across the series. The only week when he did not receive the highest number of public votes was the very first one, when Mary Byrne won after singing 'It's a Man's Man's Man's World'. Her victory was perhaps a mirror image of the support for Susan Boyle in the previous year's *Britain's Got Talent* – a vote for the middle-aged female singer. Like Susan, Mary – with her hard-working and humble background – was a great story.

Simon had seen and heard enough from young girl fans to believe his gut instinct about One Direction had been entirely correct. He also confided to Konnie Huq that Harry was his favourite member of the group: 'I'm drawn to him. I just think he gets it. He is charming and the easiest to talk to.'

The young man himself wasn't feeling too charming the following week when he felt ill as they were preparing for their sound check. They were due to perform Kelly Clarkson's 'My Life Would Suck Without You'. Nobody was sure at first if it was something he ate or just what is simplistically known as stage fright. He would later reveal that it was chronic anxiety brought on by being constantly scared he would sing a wrong note: 'I felt so much weight in terms of not getting anything wrong. I felt like if I'd sung I would have been sick.' He had to take time out and go back to the *X Factor* house to relax and eventually be given the all-clear by the show's medical advisors.

Savan revealed that everyone was worried about him but that it turned out to be an attack of nerves. In the end he coped well, although once again he didn't have any solo lines. A pattern seemed to have been established that Liam would sing the opening verse – rather like Shane Filan in Westlife – before the others came in. For this song, Zayn was the other soloist, so Harry only had to belt out the catchy chorus.

The audition scruffiness had completely disappeared. Each of the boys now had an immaculate haircut styled by Adam Reed, as well as clothes that better suited them. On a television show like *The X Factor*, how you looked was just as important as how you sounded, at least in the beginning rounds.

Their look impressed Cheryl, now happily restored to good health after her bout of malaria, who said, 'I can't even cope with how cute you are.' Simon Cowell was delighted, claiming pompously, 'You are the most exciting pop band in the country today,' which was not exactly what the remaining groups wanted to hear, especially as both Diva Fever and Belle Amie were in the bottom two, with the former going home.

The third week took in the orchestrated hysteria of a trip to Topshop in Oxford Street where hordes of girls shouted 'I love you' at them. During the show, they sang 'Nobody Knows' by Pink, a ballad that brought Harry more to the fore with a solo, although once again the trusted formula of Liam beginning the lead vocal worked well. The judges were enthusiastic and Cheryl declared the band was 'her guilty pleasure'. A few years later, in 2017, she would give birth to Liam's son, Bear.

More significantly, Louis Tomlinson revealed a significant characteristic of Harry that could easily have been ignored in the context of boys having a laugh. He knew when to work and when to play. 'He knows where the line is,' said Louis.

Unsurprisingly, the media ran stories about possible flings between contestants. Harry was linked with Cher Lloyd, arguably the most interesting and individual of the acts that season. Harry put their friendship into perspective: 'If anyone talks to anyone on *The X Factor* they are immediately dating.'

Matt Cardle, still readily winning the series, was reported to have been caught in bed with singer Katie Waissel. He was far from delighted at the stories, although such unfounded rumours generated more publicity for the show. Zayn, meanwhile, was said to be dating Geneva Lane, one of the members of Belle Amie. Niall faced rumours about him and another member of that girl group, Sophie Hardman.

Harry would have to get used to rumours of romances, true and false, as interest in the group grew. Time was up, however, for Belle Amie, who didn't make it past Halloween-themed week four. Their exit left One Direction as the only group standing. That suited Simon Cowell, who could then focus completely on their development.

Belle Amie were not happy at the lack of attention they had received. Sophie observed, 'You could put the boys out there in bin bags and sing "Baa Baa Black Sheep" and they'd go through with flying colours.'

Even Louis Walsh noticed that Simon had all but abandoned the girls. He told them, 'You've got a problem because you're on your own in this competition.' The other issue for the girls was that they didn't really get on. The show's stylist, Grace Woodward, observed, 'I feel Belle Amie are pulling in different directions. They are four solo girls and I am not sure they have gelled well enough.'

It was the Hear'Say scenario repeating itself. Matt Cardle noticed it and predicted they would split up within a few months because they 'simply do not get on well enough'. He was right – Geneva left the group after Christmas.

Fortunately, that was not going to happen to One Direction anytime soon, although there was an ironic reminder for Harry that he had actually abandoned his first group, White Eskimo; he suggested 1D sing 'Summer of '69' in the quarter-finals. *The X Factor* was no Battle of the Bands, but they performed it slickly and exuberantly, more in the style of *Glee* than Green Day. The noise from the audience was deafening. Simon pointed out that the choice had been Harry's idea, just another hint that the youngest member of the group was the 'natural frontman'.

Their second choice that night was the wonderfully soppy Joe Cocker classic 'You Are So Beautiful', a performance that revealed how much they had improved vocally during the weeks on the show thanks to some rigorous coaching. Their performance followed the established order of Liam leading, Zayn singing a solo and Harry doing the same. Perhaps a song with 'beautiful' in the title might work for the band in the future, if they secured a record deal.

More immediately, Harry topped the UK charts for the first time when the contestants joined together to record the *X Factor*'s annual charity single. This year it was a version of David Bowie's evocative 'Heroes'. Sales would benefit Help for Heroes, which provides lifelong support for military personnel bearing the scars of war and had already raised more than £70 million for wounded soldiers since it was set up in 2007.

The song was recorded while Belle Amie were still on the show, so at least they shared in the kudos of its success. Sales in the first week alone topped 144,000 copies. Matt Cardle and Rebecca Ferguson had the key roles singing the opening, revealing the producers knew back in October that they were the two who would be the frontrunners in the whole competition.

Harry had one line – 'Nothing could keep us together' – and would have been pleased not to have 'got anything wrong', but the most striking aspect of the collective performance was how good they all were. They had outstanding voices; Aiden Grimshaw, Treyc Cohen and Paije Richardson were just three of the finalists who demonstrated that it was a very thin line between success and failure on the show.

* * *

Holmes Chapel had never seen anything like it. Hundreds of screaming young fans gathered outside Harry's house in London Road, shouting 'Harry, Harry, Harry', hoping to catch a glimpse of their local hero. What a change it was from earlier in the year when they could have caught him shuffling along the street to school or to and from work. They could have queued behind him in the Chinese take-away, but those days were gone forever now that he was a bonafide pop star on the telly.

He rolled up to the front door in a limousine with blacked-out windows. Niall, Liam, Louis and Zayn were with him and they signed autographs while Harry gave his mum the biggest hug under a homemade banner that declared, 'One Direction to the Final'. He said all the right things to the press: 'I can't believe the number of people outside. It's amazing. Every week we are in total disbelief that we have got through.'

The group found time to make a 'surprise' visit to the W. Mandeville bakery. Security had already checked that it was safe for the five boys to enter unseen and be filmed. They chatted to Simon Wakefield who had made his special brunch pasties just for them.

For the final, the producers played it very safe with One Direction. First, they sang 'Your Song', which is about as daring a choice as 'Isn't She Lovely'. Liam and Harry had the solo verses and made no mistakes, but it did seem a pity to perform another Elton song. He had been the theme of the show just four weeks earlier when they had chosen the schmaltzy 'Something About the Way You Look Tonight'.

More excitingly their star duet was with Robbie Williams, until then the ultimate example of a successful solo career after boy-band fame, at least in the UK. Robbie is almost exactly twenty years older than Harry and was also sixteen when he joined Take That as their youngest member. He walked on after Liam and Harry had sung the opening verses of his number one 'She's the One' and looked a million dollars. Robbie is a big bloke and his stage presence did make the boys appear like the teenagers they were, but it was a performance to bring a smile to the faces of the most cynical. The boys themselves were clearly delighted and Simon confirmed that 'it was the night of their lives'.

The noise in the theatre was completely deafening, especially when Dermot spoke to Harry, who was centre stage in an elegant purple suit that was a step up from his hoodie. Intriguingly, Robbie has always employed a slight mid-Atlantic twang to his singing voice – a characteristic that might suit Harry looking forward. With hindsight, the song would have better complemented the sweeter, clearer tones of Zayn, but One Direction still made the final three, alongside Matt and Rebecca, who remained firm favourites, in that order. Afterwards Robbie advised them to be nice to everyone they meet and to stay away from drugs.

The following night was their final performance and they sang 'Torn', which, again, was unadventurous as the audience had already seen them sing that at Judges' Houses. Apparently the boys were particularly keen to revisit the song, but it seemed lightweight alongside Matt Cardle's interpretation of Katy Perry's 'Firework' and Rebecca doing her best Annie Lennox for 'Sweet Dreams (Are Made of This)'. Despite the noisy appreciation of One Direction from the live audience, they only received half the votes that Matt did.

One Direction were eliminated and so forfeited the chance to perform their 'winner's song', a quite obscure eighties' track called 'Forever Young' by the German synth band Alphaville. That was a pity as its anthemic quality suited them and became an enduring favourite during their future concerts.

Matt won, unsurprisingly, and his song 'When We Collide' would be UK number one in the blink of an eye. Although they never placed higher than third on any show, the boys could not contain their disappointment. It's the nature of competition that you always think you have a chance of beating Usain Bolt if you are in the race.

This seventh season was *The X Factor*'s finest hour. More than 17.7 million viewers switched on for the final alone, making it the most-watched TV show of the year. The following year the figure for the final, won by Little Mix, had slumped to a little over 12 million. That may have had something to do with Simon, Cheryl and Dannii taking a break from judging duties.

The rumours had been flying around that Simon planned to sign One Direction to his Syco label, now part of the Sony group. They were true. After the show had finished and before everyone gathered for the afterparty, he told the boys the good news. The deal was reputed to be worth £1 million, or some said £2 million – although that's a figure that makes an enticing headline. In reality, he had given each of them an early Christmas present of £8,000. The only downside was that the contract wouldn't be confirmed until the morning.

Harry was in tears but couldn't share the happy news, not even with his mum and Robin, who were there to support him on the night. He acknowledged, 'If this works out, it's going to totally change my life.'

6

NUMBER ONE
DIRECTION

———

Harry realised he had arrived when the Jack Wills store in Covent Garden rang up and asked if he would like to wear one of their t-shirts on *The X Factor*. 'I'll be in tomorrow,' said Harry, chuffed to bits. It was the first time he had been asked to wear anything, although it would not be long before designers were queuing up to invite him to model their latest creations. His life as a celebrity was beginning.

Part of the *X Factor* journey is turning unknowns into celebrities by taking them out into the world. One week One Direction would be at the Pride of Britain Awards at the Grosvenor House Hotel in Park Lane, the next being interviewed on the red carpet at the premiere of *Harry Potter and the Deathly Hallows: Part 1* at the iconic Odeon, Leicester Square.

Interest in them did not wane when the show was over. In fact, the opposite was true, as the band was surrounded by mounting hysteria wherever they went. Ronan Keating couldn't believe his eyes when he arrived at Heathrow Airport on a flight from Los Angeles and was greeted by hundreds of screaming young girl fans. It was pandemonium. They weren't there for the Boyzone heartthrob, though. He observed wistfully, 'Sadly not for me. Ha ha! One Direction were on the flight ... Those were the days.'

To be fair to Ronan, Boyzone had been a huge boy band in the nineties and he had become part of the group at sixteen, the same age as Harry when he joined 1D. He had watched fellow Irish band Westlife overtake him in the fast lane, and now it was the turn of the next big thing. He was only thirty-three but a veteran in pop terms.

Ronan had been in the States to record with the legendary Burt Bacharach. One Direction was there to shake hands, be sociable and introduce themselves to those who might be important to them as Simon Cowell prepared to launch their US career. He wanted them to meet top songwriters and producers and spread the word that they were in the market for a substantial record deal in the States.

Christmas had been a quiet time for Harry back in Cheshire, a chance to recharge batteries and spend some quality time with his family. He caught up with old buddies including Will and Nick, but was disappointed to discover some friends treated him differently, perhaps simply jealous or waiting for him to act superior. One disgruntled classmate described him as an 'arrogant prick'.

After that rural interlude, visiting Los Angeles for the first time was exciting. They stayed at the W Hotel in West Beverly Hills, conveniently close to the fashionable boutiques of Rodeo Drive. They were driven a couple of miles away for a photo opportunity at The Grove, the scenic Hollywood shopping precinct in Fairfax District, which, at the time, boasted an Abercrombie & Fitch flagship store. That suited Harry, who still loved a t-shirt with a logo on it. He raced around like a child in the candy store at Christmas. Louis joked that he had bought every t-shirt in the place. Harry did sheepishly admit that he had grabbed quite a few.

More significantly for the future, they were introduced to some key people in their recording future. Producers could listen to them in the studio and form some ideas of how they might sound for the vital first record. The weeks were about to pass very quickly so plans needed to be made early.

They laid down some early tracks with some of the current Swedish kings of chart music. Leading producers including RedOne, Carl Falk and Rami Yacoub were much in demand, dividing their time between LA and Stockholm. They had developed their expertise in the footsteps of Max Martin, the grandmaster of Swedish pop. Rami, for instance, had worked with Max at his Cheiron Studios in Stockholm on some of the best-known hits of recent years, including '... Baby One More Time' and 'Oops! ... I Did it Again' for Britney Spears and many songs for Backstreet Boys and Westlife.

One Direction had dinner with Max and he was happy to pass on some tips. They met up with Cher Lloyd, who had also been shipped off to LA to make a start on her album. She was photographed strolling around The Grove with the boys. Harry was sporting a newly purchased polo shirt with the A&C logo. For a while Cher's career progressed in tandem with One Direction as she too was working with RedOne and other Swedish producers including Shellback and Savan Kotecha from *The X Factor*, who was a well-respected song-writer in his own right.

Quite clearly, the plan was to start One Direction at the very top. Time was blocked off in their diary to travel to Stockholm, to work more seriously on their debut album. The first commitment, however, was back in the UK for the annual *X Factor* tour. This was a Simon Cowell money-spinning exercise that was expected to raise upwards of £10 million by the time merchandise and all the spin–offs were added to ticket sales.

They didn't have long to rehearse before the opening night at Birmingham's LG Arena in February. Fortunately, they had already learned their set during the *X Factor* series: Rihanna's 'Only Girl (in the World)'; the elegiac classic 'Chasing Cars' by Snow Patrol; 'Kids in America', the Kim Wilde oldie from 1981; Kelly Clarkson's 'My Life Would Suck Without You'; and finally 'Forever Young', the winner's song they didn't have the chance to perform in the final. They were allotted five songs, the same as the actual winner Matt Cardle.

The front of the programme featured prominently the four acts that Simon Cowell had signed to Syco. He may have envisaged One Direction as the potential superstars, but he had taken the precaution of also giving contracts to Cher Lloyd, Matt Cardle and Rebecca Ferguson, who were pictured across the top with the five members of One Direction occupying the next row. Harry was in the middle.

The reviews of the tour were very mixed, although the *Belfast Telegraph* noted that One Direction was the 'young boy band with a big future'. The *Independent* described their reception from the audience as 'supersonic'.

When the show reached Wembley Arena, the *Guardian* critic Michael Cragg was perhaps not entirely empathetic with the thousands of young girls who were only there to shout, scream and swoon at One Direction. He observed, 'The noise levels go beyond human hearing capabilities for One Direction, an old-school boy band who only ever seem to harmonise by accident.' He was complimentary about Cher, Rebecca and Aidan Grimshaw, with whom Harry had always got on well; this was their last chance to catch up before they took very different career paths. Matt closed the show and Michael suggested pessimistically that Matt should 'enjoy it while it lasts'.

The nine acts returned to the stage to perform their charity number one, 'Heroes'. By the end of the year One Direction would have eclipsed them all.

When the tour ended at the Motorpoint Arena in Cardiff in mid-April, there was a week for a short break before recording the first album would begin in earnest. Harry went skiing with Louis and a couple of mates to Courchevel, in the French Alps. He hadn't skied before so he relied on his bandmate to help with basic technique – namely not falling over and breaking a leg.

Harry and Louis were the closest among the five members of One Direction. It helped that their mums had become firm friends as they watched their sons achieve fame so quickly. Both Anne and Jay combined to create a public platform to promote the causes about which they felt most strongly.

The boys also decided to share a luxury apartment in the suburb of Friern Barnet, just north of London. They moved into a flat in Princess Park Manor, named in honour of Princess Diana, which was home to many pop stars and footballers over the years. Simon Cowell's company, Syco, had a deal with the property developers that he could house his artists in the building that had been converted from a Victorian mental hospital. The rent was £5,000 a month.

The advantage of the secure location was that celebrities could come and go without having the prying lenses of paparazzi snapping them every time they went for a swim or popped to the tennis courts. The other three boys also moved into the Manor, but the luxury complex is so big that you might never meet another tenant.

Louis and Harry's new home used to be occupied by the England footballer Ashley Cole, who lived there while his eventual wife, *X Factor* judge Cheryl, shared another flat with Girls Aloud bandmate Nicola Roberts. By chance Ashley had spotted Cheryl when she walked by one day when he was visiting a friend in another apartment. She recalled, 'I walked past and he shouted, "Hey hot lips." I hate stuff like that so I rolled my eyes and was like, "Piss off."' It was a start. That opener from Ashley, though, was not in the Harry Styles dictionary of chat-up lines.

Living with Louis was an early indication that Harry much preferred sharing with other people than being on his own. For the moment he had to fly out to Stockholm to begin serious work on their debut album. Harry stood out when they started recording at the Kinglet Studios in Stockholm; not because he was a better singer than the others, he was just different. Carl Falk explained, 'He's got a very raspy voice. It's a good compliment to have to some of the others who are a bit more "clean". Harry brings a raspy, raw character to the recording process.'

Carl had nothing but praise for the band's work ethic, each of whom were taking everything very seriously. He reflected, 'They listen to what we say and our suggestions and there's never been an argument or any bullshit with them.'

The very first track they worked on was one that Savan Kotecha had brought in. Harry was in no doubt when he heard the early demo that it was perfect for their debut single. He sent Savan a text message that read simply, 'I think you got it. I think you got the one here.' He was right: 'What Makes You Beautiful' was perfect – the sweet sentiments of a romantic ballad dressed up in an infectious danceable rhythm. Savan was so chuffed he kept the text.

He had first thought of the catchy melody the previous year but needed inspiration for the lyrics. That came unexpectedly one day when he and his wife were staying at the five-star Royal Garden Hotel, close to Hyde Park. He was in the bathroom when he heard his Swedish wife, Anna Gustavsson, complaining that she felt so ugly that morning.

He shouted out, 'No you're not!' and had a lightbulb moment that he later explained, 'I was thinking "Wow, one of the great things about you is that you don't know how beautiful you are and that's what makes you beautiful."' He wrote the thought down before he left to go to the studio and shared it with Carl and Rami, as well as the original melody to the line, 'Baby you light up my world like nobody else.' It's easy to see how romantic old Harry would love the sentiment.

Both Carl and Rami loved it too, not just a 'beautiful' title but a 'really smart concept' that teenagers would appreciate. They set about finding the right sound for One Direction – an updated version of the original Swedish melodies of the nineties that had provided huge hits for the Backstreet Boys, NSYNC and Britney.

They were concerned, however, that the music that had been so popular in that decade would appear dated for a new generation, so they ditched the synths and pianos and replaced them with good old-fashioned guitars. They weren't looking to make Eric Clapton or Jimmy Page jealous, however. Carl Falk explained, 'The guitar riff had to be so simple that my friend's fifteen-year-old daughter could play it and put her cover up on YouTube.'

Their strategy worked perfectly with 'What Makes You Beautiful'. The two-finger guitar intro was copied in a million bedrooms. The trio of Swedish maestros crafted three songs for the album. As well as the first composition, they co-wrote and produced 'I Wish' and 'One Thing', which was originally two songs – one had a good verse, the other a winning chorus. They merged them together. Carl thought it was actually a better song than 'What Makes You Beautiful'.

When Roisin O'Connor, the *Independent*'s music writer, ranked all ninety-six songs in the 1D catalogue, she placed 'One Thing' at number five, by far the highest position of any track from the first album. She called it a 'preppier version' of 'I Want It That Way', which was no bad thing as the Backstreet Boys' signature song reached number one all around the world, including in the UK, in 1999.

The *X Factor* shows and subsequent tour did not prepare One Direction for life in the studio. Carl observed, 'They were searching for themselves.' Despite being the most affected by pre-stage nerves, Harry was brimming with confidence in the recording booth. He was up for anything and they could have just recorded him, which would have ruined the concept of a boy band. The most important thing was that they were all willing to learn and improve.

Sweden did not have a monopoly on the album, although RedOne also contributed two tracks. Harry was keen to involve other songwriters to prevent the album from becoming too samey. He asked Ed Sheeran if he had any songs he wanted to put up. They had been introduced by one of Ed's collaborators, the guitarist Chris Leonard. As ever, Ed was always happy to write songs for other acts. He always had songs. He enjoyed a process that improved his profile in the days before he became a one-man pop juggernaut.

Ed popped in to see Tyler Brown, then head of A&R at Syco, and left some tracks for consideration. They included a song called 'Moments' that he had written some time before with another collaborator, Si Hulbert, who was horrified when Ed told him he had included it: 'It was probably the shoddiest demo I had ever done with him if I'm honest. It actually started off as a drum and bass track.'

Ed was busy with promotion when Tyler emailed to say they wanted it. He also suggested how it could be reworked. Si recalled, 'Basically I totally changed it into a boy band sort of epic ballad.' One concern Si had was whether the content was suitable for a boy band. 'Moments' was actually inspired by the sad death, aged fifteen, of his younger sister. The poignant lyric is about missing her: 'If I could only have this life for one more day.'

Si once asked Ed Sheeran if One Direction knew what the song was about and he replied that he didn't think so. It didn't matter because it was a track that you could relate to personally in different ways. 'If you are a fourteen-year-old girl, it's about losing your boyfriend.'

As was customary, Liam sang the opening solo. His voice suited songs that began in a lower register. Harry would then provide a striking contrast, singing the bridge into the often anthemic chorus. 'Moments' did not make the final listing on the album but was a bonus track and available on deluxe editions worldwide. Louis, whose solo was particularly melancholic, said it was by far his favourite track on their first album. The song is also one of the most cherished among devoted One Direction fans, performed by the boys on all three of their world tours.

That would be in the future, though. The next task in this year's masterplan was making the video for 'What Makes You Beautiful'. So they literally flew in and out of Los Angeles to film on the beautiful beach in Malibu. The director was John Urbano, who didn't have a long history of pop videos but had already been chosen as the photographer for their first album cover. The result was an impressive depiction of the sheer energy and vitality of One Direction.

The video was more of the same – a three-minute frolic splashing about in the waves with three lovely young women. Harry, in particular, turned on the megawatt charm for one of them, aspiring actress and model Madison McMillin. Days out filming pop videos were just part of trying to get ahead for someone like Madison. She was like the girl next door, not dissimilar to Jennifer Aniston in *Friends* and, as such, more relatable to the thousands of teenage girls who dreamt of being serenaded by Harry Styles.

At least the actress didn't suggest there was anything between her and Harry. That innuendo was left to Alan Carr when the boys appeared on his television show *Chatty Man*, at the start of their promotional campaign for the single. Harry had mumbled that the girls in the video were 'lovely', whereupon a picture of Madison appeared behind him and Alan asked, 'So Harry, what happened between you and Madison? Did you take a trip down Madison Avenue?' Everyone laughed at the joke, which Madison must have heard a thousand times and more.

The band was always asked about girls, literally in every interview from the very first one on *The Alan Titchmarsh Show*, an affable afternoon chat on ITV. In the recent past, the strategy was always to make sure the fan base thought the boy band was available. Take That, for example, had to smuggle their secret girlfriends into hotels when they were touring.

Simon Cowell appeared completely relaxed about girls as far as One Direction was concerned. He declared that he was not a Svengali-type figure lecturing the boys on what they could or could not do: 'If I were their age in this group, I'd want to have a good time.' He also confirmed that all the boys liked girls.

That sounded good when it was banter about Madison or when Harry pointed out that his dream girl was Frankie Sandford of The Saturdays, who was twenty-one and gamely played along by suggesting she would date him if he was older.

At this stage, nobody had taken seriously Harry's actual preference for older women. While he was happy to embrace some light-hearted larks, he kept completely quiet about a real fling he was having. The woman in question was married, fourteen years his senior and a popular radio personality.

He met Lucy Horobin when the band popped in for a promotional chat at the Key 103 Radio station in Manchester. While she played the record, he flirted in Harry fashion, held his heart and mouthed 'I love you' to her. They kept in touch on social media and by text and met up again when he was back in Manchester in September.

Lucy is a brunette with a winning smile, rather reminiscent of Harry's mum. She didn't breathe a word about their relationship, and neither did he. The world would never have known that they hooked up again after an Ed Sheeran concert if it hadn't been for her estranged husband spilling the beans to a tabloid newspaper the following summer.

By the end of 2011, however, Harry had embarked on something more serious with a more famous broadcaster, born the same year as Lucy. The relationship would become his most notorious and one that was forever tinged with sadness.

PART TWO

HARRY & CO.

7

AN INNOCENT
RELATIONSHIP

When Harry was snapped by paparazzi leaving Caroline Flack's North London home on a wintry morning in early December 2011, it would change his life – and hers – forever. Until then, his blossoming relationship with the new host of *The Xtra Factor* had been the subject of light tittle-tattle in the newspapers but now it faced the full glare of vitriolic opinion.

Harry had first flirted with the popular television personality back in August when he told the official *X Factor* website, 'If Caroline Flack is reading this, say "Hi" from me. She is gorgeous.' Subsequently, he enlisted the help of one of the producers to send DM messages on Twitter to Caroline, letting her know that he was up for a date.

She was flattered and amused in equal measure. Harry was seventeen and she was thirty-one, three weeks older than Lucy Horobin. The age gap bothered neither of them. In her autobiography, *Storm in a C Cup*, Caroline memorably described him as 'a man/boy with a captivating smile who got what he wanted'.

Like Harry, Caroline, or Carrie as her family called her, was brought up in rural surroundings. Although she and her twin sister, Jo, were born in Enfield, they moved to the quiet village of Great Hocking, in Norfolk, aged four when her father was promoted to a management job with Coca-Cola that gave him responsibility for the whole of the county.

They moved again when Caroline was seven, to the more remote village of East Wretham, to the north of Thetford Forest. They were a family of six and needed more space. Caroline and Jo had an elder brother and sister, Paul and Elizabeth. The setting for their new home was an idyllic slice of Breckland landscape, but Caroline dreamed of a life on the stage.

She was very petite and slim as a child and her 'absolute idol' was Kylie Minogue. The twins would be glued to the telly every night watching *Neighbours* after getting in from school. Later on, their party piece was singing 'Especially for You' in the lounge, when Caroline played Kylie and Jo was Jason Donovan.

Caroline went to secondary school in Watton, ten miles away. She thought the market town was a dump, was excruciatingly bored and couldn't wait to get away. Salvation came when her childhood dance classes paid off and she was given a bursary to attend the Bodywork Dance School in Cambridge. She was there from the age of seventeen until she was twenty.

Moving to London, she was working at the Medicine Bar in Islington when she made her movie debut playing a tiny role in a made-for-TV film called, ironically, *Is Harry on the Boat?* This is an obscure cockney rhyming slang reference to spunk on the face – Harry Monk, Boat Race. Caroline, and the majority of those who saw the comedy-drama about holiday reps, had no idea that was the meaning.

Caroline's character didn't have a name. She was just on the cast list as 'Blonde'. The film wasn't porn in the slightest, although she did have to go topless. Blink and you miss her in a scene with the star, Danny Dyer. The big plus was a week's filming in Ibiza.

Her moment on screen did not lead to a flood of offers. Instead, she won a role alongside Leigh Francis in his ribald sketch show *Bo' Selecta!* In the days before he rebranded himself as Keith Lemon, Leigh would dress up as various pop stars and indulge in some outrageous behaviour. When he pretended to be Michael Jackson, Caroline was his glamorous assistant Bubbles, in a low-cut top and shorts, an outfit the tabloids would describe as 'raunchy'.

The show hasn't aged well and Leigh would later apologise for his portrayal of black people, calling it 'offensive'. Caroline called him a mentor and a friend, 'He is gentle, supportive and honest. He watches everything I do and will say if I was brilliant or not too good. Leigh is the opposite of what he's like when he's in character, which is really ballsy.'

To a certain extent that was true of Caroline herself as she moved up the television ladder, improving her profile presenting shows including a revival of the hit eighties' series *Gladiators* and *Big Brother's Big Mouth*. Her biggest show was *I'm a Celebrity, Get Me Out of Here! NOW!*, the companion to the Ant and Dec's ratings blockbuster *I'm a Celebrity, Get Me Out of Here!*, probably the only one that could rival the popularity of *The X Factor*.

The annual trip to New South Wales was a dream job for any presenter – escaping the British winter and not having to engage in any Bushtucker Trials. She also met a fellow presenter making a name for herself in television. Dawn Porter, as she was then, was the same age and the two women became best friends. Dawn recalled, 'We laughed all week, told each other everything and bonded for life. The absolute greatest of times.'

Behind the façade of success, however, Caroline struggled to handle criticism, especially when the media sharpened their knives. She first faced the full glare of media scrutiny when it was revealed she was dating Prince Harry. They had met at a club in Chelsea in 2009. All she would say on the matter was, 'I was photographed with him and we did have a friendship.'

Caroline was totally unprepared for the onslaught from the Sunday papers. One front-page headline shouted, 'Harry's Girl in Three-in-a-Tub romp'. The source of the story was an unnamed 'pal'. Caroline, it claimed, was a 'wild child party animal' who once 'romped' in a tub with Sharon Osbourne's son Jack. Female celebrities, it seems, are always going to be targeted with this sort of headline. Before she became a national treasure, Cheryl woke up to the *News of the World* shouting, 'I Had Rub-a-Dub in the Tub with Girls Aloud Cheryl'.

Nothing seemed to change. It was depressingly similar to the headline the first week Meghan Markle was revealed as Prince Harry's new girlfriend. That read: 'Harry's Girl on Pornhub'. A subsequent apology does not cancel the original story.

As well as the scrutiny she herself received, Caroline's entire family was door-stepped and investigated. Again, it was very similar to the methods used six years later in Meghan's case, with so-called representatives of the papers sent out with chequebooks ready. According to Caroline, all her Facebook friends were offered money 'for dirt'.

Prince Harry understood the pressures any woman would face if they were linked to him. He was not photographed with Caroline again. Caroline explained that they had to stop seeing each other because neither wanted to face that level of press intrusion. Sadly, it would not be the last time she made the front pages for a relationship.

Caroline later revealed that she lost two stone in weight and would spend hours alone in her North London flat, just crying. The other famous Harry was blissfully unaware of such dramas, studying for his GCSEs in Holmes Chapel. He didn't meet Caroline during his time on *The X Factor*. She had gone up for the job as presenter of *The Xtra Factor* but had lost out to Konnie Huq. She had impressed Simon Cowell, however, and he took her on the following year when Konnie decided not to return.

To begin with, the rumours were flying that she was involved with co-presenter Olly Murs – nothing to see there. The reality was that she and Harry had got together after meeting up at an *X Factor* party at the W Hotel in Leicester Square. They were seen having a snog and left together.

While the media were fascinated by Caroline's love life involving the two Harrys and other possible or probable romances, she had been involved in an on-off relationship with drummer Dave Danger from the indie band The Holloways. That was over by the time she began dating Harry Styles, who tweeted, 'Sometimes things happen and you suddenly get a whole new outlook on life.' To begin with, it seemed like no big deal to the media – they would just make the odd comment about Harry already having an eye for the older woman.

The following month, in September 2011, 'What Makes You Beautiful' went straight to number one in the UK, selling more than 150,000 copies in its first week of release. They had a little way to go to match Adele, who was the queen of the charts with 'Someone Like You' and 'Rolling in the Deep', but the track crept into the top twenty of the biggest-selling singles of the year; it ended up with sales of more than a million and remains their biggest ever hit.

Its success was the final piece in the jigsaw for One Direction before they signed a lucrative American contract with Columbia Records, who were already enjoying great success across the Atlantic with Adele. British boy bands had not done particularly well in the US up until that point, but the record label could see a gap in the market left by the disbanded Backstreet Boys and NSYNC.

While the campaign for One Direction in the UK had been very old school, the American strategy was more modern, tapping into social media and the internet. The approach was groundbreaking and One Direction was arguably the first act to properly cash in online.

The problem with harnessing social media to generate publicity and commercial success was that the platforms made it very difficult for celebrities like One Direction to enjoy any privacy without the whole world seemingly having a view on what you, your friends or your lovers were up to.

Caroline and Harry had been seeing each other for a month before One Direction were guest stars on *The X Factor* performing their second single, 'Gotta Be You', in mid-November. By the time the band sang 'What Makes You Beautiful' during the December final, the rules of the game had completely changed.

It was the previous week that Harry had been photographed leaving Caroline's Muswell Hill flat early one Wednesday morning. In the subsequent stories, Harry was described as a 'school leaver', leaving no room for doubt as to the direction the press accounts were going to take.

References were made to him arriving the night before, having an overnight bag and looking tired the next day. The press were tying themselves up in knots to avoid stating categorically that Harry had clearly been up all night having sex.

In her own memoir, Caroline would lay the blame for the social media backlash at the door of the columnist Jan Moir, who next day in the *Daily Mail* described Caroline as a 'classic me-first cougar' and a 'predatory female', while Harry was 'basically still a child'. Jan highlighted the age gap: 'No wonder people find their liaison inappropriate; even slightly creepy.'

Caroline concluded, 'Once that was out, it was open season.' Passers-by felt empowered to shout out to her in the street: 'Paedophile' or 'Pervert'.

Jan had also suggested, 'And I don't imagine his mother is best pleased with these rather off-key romantic developments with a predatory older woman.'

In fact, Anne and Caroline were following each other on Twitter and Harry's mum had wished her a happy birthday earlier in November. Harry had taken Caroline to Cheshire to meet his mother and stepfather and, in turn, he had met her family. Her sister Jo was even spotted dropping him at King's Cross station to catch a train north.

For a while they tried to ride out the media storm but it seemed everyone had an opinion on whether the age gap made the relationship unsuitable. Anne, who was ten years younger than Harry's father, was calm about everything: 'I never really thought it would be a problem,' she said, before adding, 'Personality is more important than anything else.'

Des Styles, apparently, was less enthusiastic: 'It seemed a bit ridiculous – thirty-two or whatever she was and Harry seventeen. That's a bit extreme.' In his defence, Des did point out that he had been married three times 'so I wouldn't say anyone should take a leaf out of my book'.

Old friend Will Sweeny was asked about it. He observed, 'All his mates think he is a bit of a legend. It's classic Styles.'

Caroline and Harry went to see her agent, John Noel, for some advice and, for the moment, they decided to ignore the newspaper and social-media storm. In effect, that just prolonged the agony and made her a daily target. One Direction already had security and a private living environment. Caroline, however, lived in a maisonette that opened onto the street.

She opened the door in the morning and was greeted by a flurry of flashbulbs. On one morning she went across to the car and discovered that her tyres had been slashed. Nobody offered to help her. At Christmas, Caroline whisked herself off to the beautiful destination of Goa on the coast of India for a girls' holiday with Dawn Porter and others. Harry posted a tweet on 22 December that said simply, 'Work Hard, Play Hard, Be Kind.'

Only one or two people were being kind about him and Caroline. She faced a barrage of death threats, some more sinister than others. One message hoped that she would be 'eaten by an angry elephant'.

In January they tried to pick things up again, but the pressure became too much and they decided to call it a day. Harry was due to fly with the band to the US, so there was a chance for a natural break. There was an air of jubilation among fans, so much so that Harry was again moved to write on Twitter: 'Please know I didn't "dump" Caroline. This was a mutual decision. She is one of the kindest, sweetest people I know. Please respect that.'

Significantly, this is the one and only time that Harry has taken to Twitter to defend or even comment on a former girlfriend. Caroline was brittle as well as beautiful. She somehow never learned the art of saying nothing. A couple of months later she told a Sunday newspaper that Harry was adorable and that they were 'very close' for a time. She added, 'He is a nice person. He was nice to me – we were nice to each other. He's brilliant, he is so much fun.'

In 2021 her other Harry – Prince Harry – produced a series of programmes about mental health called *The Me You Can't See*. That certainly applied to Caroline, who left us in February 2020. She once said that celebrities expected there to be photographers at a public event because it was their job. It was an entirely different thing when 'they turn up at your mum's house, and when you are driving down your street and you have to swerve because there are three cars behind you and three motorbikes following you wherever you go'.

She said stoically, 'I have my dream job so I can't complain. If it got too much I would give it up, so obviously it hasn't got too much.'

Quietly, Caroline received support from an unexpected quarter. There had been some speculation that Simon Cowell had been less than pleased that a member of One Direction was involved with an older woman. That was not the case. He had been astounded, though, by the sequence of events involving his teenage 'frontman'.

Coincidentally Simon was himself seventeen years older than Lauren Silverman, the American socialite who gave birth to his son Eric in February 2014. Two years earlier, at the afterparty of the BRIT Awards, he went up to Caroline to check if she would be hosting *The Xtra Factor* again later in the year. He told her, 'I'd like to apologise for the way you were treated.'

The affection between Caroline and Harry during their three months together was real, if not exactly true love. In many ways, it was an innocent relationship. He had bought himself a swish Audi R8 Coupé, the perfect car for driving up to see his mum in Cheshire. On the journey, he would pop on a CD that Caroline had made of their favourite songs, a simple, romantic gesture that was something personal just for him; and he would sing along. It was a happy reminder of her and the music they enjoyed listening to at her flat.

One consequence of what happened between Harry and Caroline was that he retreated. Both would have more important relationships in the future but the scars from this one ran deep. Harry became secretive when not on official duty at those public events that Caroline mentioned or when he was out and about with fellow celebrities. He did not engage with tabloid media, preferring to give big exclusive interviews to publications he trusted. Nobody even knew where he lived!

8

CONNECTIONS

———

On his eighteenth birthday, Harry decided to do something for the first time: He was now old enough to vote, open a bank account, serve on a jury and, at least in the UK, order an alcoholic drink in a bar. He could also get a tattoo, and that was his present to himself to celebrate his coming of age.

He was in Los Angeles so he didn't have to worry about what his mum might say. Instead, he strolled into the famous Shamrock Social Club on Sunset Boulevard and asked tattoo artist Freddy Negrete to ink the outline of a five-pointed star on the inside of his left bicep.

Harry has not revealed what the star represented. One Direction fans speculated that it was a point for each member of the band, although it could also have been his personal walk of fame star, inspired by the legendary pavement in nearby Hollywood Boulevard. It was identical.

The star was a very low-key beginning for a man who now possesses more than fifty tattoos all over his body. He was in good company choosing the Shamrock; many British household names have been through the doors, including David Beckham, Russell Brand, Fearne Cotton and Adele.

Harry was back more than half a dozen times within the year, gripped by what Freddy later described as 'tattoo fever'. He explained, 'If you get a tattoo and you like it, you want more – it happens to a lot of people.'

They are also very fashionable and enduringly so. Fashion commentator Alison Jane Reid explained, 'Tattoos are all about rebellion but they are also now perceived to be an haute art form for the rich and famous.'

Harry was in the US with One Direction as part of the American strategy of embracing online coverage and social media to boost interest in the release there of 'What Makes You Beautiful' on Valentine's Day. The hype was in full swing with silly tunes and goofy posts, contests and fan petitions aimed at making the record the only tune in town. Radio stations across the country were being inundated with requests to play the song – and they didn't even have it.

In its first week the single reached number twenty-eight on the *Billboard* Hot 100 chart. That may not sound too impressive but the last British group to see its first US single debut in a higher position was the Spice Girls when their iconic 'Wannabe' made number eleven in 1997.

Just as significantly, 'What Makes You Beautiful' sold 132,000 downloads in seven days and that was before Columbia were going to make it available for radio airplay at the beginning of March. In the end-of-year round-up it was placed tenth in *Billboard*'s best-selling songs of the year.

Harry and the boys were back in London in time for the BRITs of 2012, held that year at the O2. He messed up spectacularly in the thank-you speech after One Direction had won their first major award, Best British Single, as voted for by listeners of Capital FM and iTunes users. Harry, looking immaculate in a three-piece grey suit and large black bow tie, gave a 'massive thank you' to *Radio 1*.

The bosses of Global Radio, which owns Capital, were in the audience and Harry's gaffe was not music to their ears. A planned appearance by the group at Capital in London was promptly dropped without explanation and for a day or two their music was, it seemed, not top of the station's playlist. A spokesman for the band called it an 'oversight as the boys were caught up in the excitement of winning'.

On the night, James Corden, who had become a good friend of Harry's, didn't notice and told the band, 'Go and ring your mums and tell them you'll be home late tonight.' Fortunately Harry was not the story of the evening. Notoriously, James interrupted Adele's big speech when she won Album of the Year for *21*. He was obviously embarrassed but only following instructions in his earpiece because the programme was about to overrun. As she turned to leave the stage, obviously furious, she flipped her middle finger towards a table of executives.

James's best mate, coincidentally, was the event's producer Ben Winston, a charismatic high-flyer in the world of television who had become friendly with One Direction when he began work on a film about their meteoric rise. He lived with his wife Meredith and a sweet cockapoo dog called Colin in upmarket Hampstead Garden Suburb.

Harry asked him if he could come and stay for a while. He explained that he had bought a house not far from Hampstead

Heath so it would be convenient to be close by while keeping an eye on the renovations that were under way. Then, he could move straight in.

He bought the house in a secluded cul-de-sac for an estimated £2.95 million, not bad for an eighteen-year-old. Harry would always make a point of investing part of his already growing fortune in property. His financial mantra was look after 70 per cent of every pound and be frivolous with the other 30 per cent. It helped having a father who was a financial advisor. Harry was part of the new sensible breed of pop star who put vast sums into the housing market knowing that their investment was unlikely to diminish. Ed Sheeran would do likewise and Taylor Swift already had a substantial property empire.

Ben was happy to oblige his friend. After all, it was only temporary; so he moved a mattress into the attic and told Harry to make himself comfortable. He did so for the next twenty months without the world knowing. He was able to slip in and out without running the gauntlet of photographers or fans lurking behind the bins.

Ben was popular with One Direction, who found him easy to get along with and good fun. That did not necessarily mean this new arrangement with Harry would work. Any misgivings on either side were quickly dispelled, however. Ben said simply, 'It was a really beautiful time. He is the most wonderful guy you could ever meet.' Ben and Meredith asked Harry to be godfather when they welcomed their first child, Ruby, into the world at the beginning of 2017.

This was the Harry Styles the world does not see. He does not have an entourage. He is not a cliché-driven representation of an old-style rock star, a throwback to the sex, drugs and rock-and-roll lifestyle favoured by so many in other eras. Quite simply, Harry preferred living in a stable and secure family environment with Ben, Meredith and Colin rather than going out on the town and then home to a soulless gated mansion.

He was seldom bothered by fans or press, even when he joined Ben and Meredith for a quiet meal out in a local restaurant. Ben explained that nobody really believed it was Harry so they left him alone. Occasionally Ben would see A-list stars he recognised slip unannounced up to his attic but stories of drunken nights – or passionate ones – never appeared subsequently in the press.

Harry became the youngest member of a network of close friends who are loyal and discreet. They don't gossip about each other or betray secrets. Ben, then aged thirty, was an integral part of this inner circle. His father, the medical scientist and Labour peer Professor Robert Winston, was a famous face on television, presenting many programmes, including *Child of Our Times* and the BAFTA Award-winning *The Human Body*. He is one of the few TV personalities over the years that have succeeded in making serious scientific and medical subjects accessible to the public. In the US, they call him the 'Daddy of IVF'.

The Winstons are also leading members of the Jewish community in London. Ben and Meredith were observant of the traditions that they had known throughout their lives. Friday night dinner, for instance, was the most important family occasion of the week, when Sabbath candles would be lit and families would come together.

Harry was always welcome to join them. He was respectful of their Jewish traditions, including keeping a kosher home, and was fascinated to learn more about Judaism while chatting over a hot drink before bed. Ben explained that orthodox rules such as not driving on the Sabbath were easy to follow for him because he had grown up with them and they were part of his life and lifestyle.

Ben had ambitions to follow his father into the world of television, inspired by the programmes he made. Lord Winston has always been a keen supporter of the arts and in his younger days had worked as a theatre director before embarking on medicine as his principal vocation.

During his gap year in 2000 Ben worked as a runner in Bristol on the set of a new comedy drama, *Teachers*. On his very first day, he met a young actor, James Corden, playing the role of a Year 11 pupil – although already in his twenties – who would become his closest friend as well an important figure in Harry's life. 'We instantly clicked,' said Ben. 'We recognised sheer ambition in one another.' They also both loved football, although bragging rights invariably went to Ben, who supported Arsenal, rather than James, a West Ham fan.

Their early friendship was sustained when James filmed the drama series *Fat Friends* in Leeds and would regularly hang out with Ben, who was at university there. In the world of weird showbusiness coincidences, James used to kick a foot-ball around on set with young teenager Louis Tomlinson, when he was helping his mother Jay chaperone his baby twin sisters.

Jay rang up James when Louis and Harry started living in Friern Barnet and asked if he could check that the teenage boys were coping. James spent the afternoon with them playing computer games and eating pizza and was able to report back to Mum that they were fine.

When Ben left Leeds, he moved back to London and went into partnership with three of his oldest friends, brothers Gabe and Ben Turner, and Leo Pearlman. They had grown up together from pushchairs in the park to enthusiastic members of Bnei Akiva, the UK's largest Jewish youth movement.

Their new production company was called Fulwell 73, named after the last year Sunderland won the FA Cup. The club's old Roker Park Stadium had a Fulwell End. The Turner brothers' mum and dad were from the north east, so watching all their games was compulsory growing up. From unpromising beginnings the business has grown into a resounding success story and one that would be particularly associated with One Direction and, subsequently, Harry.

The new partners had received many plaudits for their work on the 2007 documentary *In the Hands of the Gods*, about five freestyle footballers from different backgrounds in England who come together to pursue an ambition to meet their idol, Diego Maradona, in Buenos Aires. James worked with Ben again when he put his friend forward to direct the much-loved 2009 Comic Relief sketch in which Smithy, his character from hit comedy *Gavin and Stacey*, gives a rollicking to the England football team, including David Beckham and Peter Crouch.

Ben's production work on *Eyes Wide Open 3D*, a documentary about the life of *X Factor* runners-up JLS, brought him to the attention of One Direction. The two groups shared the same management company, Modest, who handled most of the show's stars. Ben met all five of 1D at the premiere at the Soho Hotel in London and instantly had a great rapport with them. As a direct result of getting on so well he embarked on the ambitious and ultimately phenomenally successful *One Direction: This Is Us*, a film that chronicled the boys' meteoric rise to fame from early *X Factor* days to Madison Square Garden in New York in December 2013. He enjoyed their company: 'We made each other laugh. They are always mucking around and there's an anarchic feel about them which makes my job much more fun.' He added, 'I look at them like they are my five little brothers.'

For television, he was the producer of both the 2011 and 2012 BRIT Awards shows at the O2 that his buddy James Corden hosted. In this very small world at the top of show-business, it was another step on the path to world domination for this unlikely duo whose rise throughout the next decade almost matched that of the pop stars James was introducing.

A couple of days before the 2012 ceremony, James was Harry's unlikely companion at the Savoy Hotel when Harry went to a London Fashion Week show for the first time without the other members of the band. James is not normally associated with sartorial elegance, but he was accompanying his glamorous fiancée Julia Carey, who he had met at a charity dinner in 2009 for Save the Children that she had helped to organise. Julia sat between the two friends in the front row of the Aquascutum runway show. Harry arrived wearing a timeless beige Aquascutum trench coat with the familiar check lining, which he placed on his lap during the show so that it was in the frame every time his picture was taken. The low-key occasion was early evidence that Harry was beginning to separate himself from the group in certain areas of his life.

They were back together in March when the US release of *Up All Night* was brought forward by a week to capitalise on the success of 'What Makes You Beautiful'. They played a one-off concert at the iconic Radio City Music Hall venue in New York, sharing the bill with the American boy band Big Time Rush, who were also signed to Columbia; they were the stars of a Nickelodeon TV series and very popular but were soon left trailing as One Direction moved towards world domination.

Columbia and Syco made the daring decision to cash in on this burst of popularity and release a second album for Christmas 2012. The boys were young, keen and fit but this would be challenging; and they were also growing up, not just obediently following the path that was being mapped out for them. They wanted a greater say in the sound and the songs they would be performing all over the world.

Savan Kotecha, Carl Falk and Rami Yacoub were again charged with setting the tone for the follow-up, which would be called *Take Me Home* – rather apt for a band that was on the road as much as One Direction was. When their schedule allowed, they would find a window to fly over to Stockholm and record again at the Kinglet Studios. This time they had writing credits on three of the songs, as well as several of the bonus tracks.

Nobody wanted to change a good thing too much so, largely, this was *Up All Night* part two. That was certainly what the record label bosses wanted, just in case the One Direction phenomenon was short-lived. That didn't look likely whenever the band were in the Swedish capital, though. On one occasion the whole street around the studio had to be shut down because of the sheer number of girls who had turned up, desperate for a glimpse of the boys. The city police even arrived clutching missing-person photos to see if any of the teenagers were runaways and had left home without telling their parents what they were doing.

Songwriters around the world were encouraged to submit their compositions for the new One Direction album. Simon Cowell put out an open invitation. Harry had already asked his new mate Ed Sheeran if he would like to offer another song. He did, and once again it became one of One Direction's most-loved songs. 'Little Things' wasn't something new and bespoke at all but a track Ed had worked on with struggling singer-songwriter Fiona Bevan. They had both wanted to write a love song and Fiona was inspired by the novelist Virginia Woolf: 'She always looked at the minutiae and emotion of a situation. I'd been thinking about that a lot, and how the little things really represent the big things.'

Ed thought it was a terrific idea. Fiona recalled, 'We were thinking of real people we loved, and the strange quirks and imperfections that made us love them. So everything in the song is real, which is a lovely thing to be able to say.'

As ever, One Direction could have been singing directly to any one of their adoring fans. That was a vital secret of their success. They had a once-in-a-lifetime knack of speaking directly to one person in a song. They could melt a million hearts when they sang, 'You're perfect to me.'

While they were absorbed in the next album, they still had a full touring diary. They began mixing with the superstars of pop, an indication that they were now in the premier league. Before they set off for Australia, Harry met Taylor Swift for the first time backstage at the Nickelodeon Kids' Choice Awards hosted by Will Smith at the USC Galen Center in Los Angeles. She was seen having a dance with her great friend, Selena Gomez, while the band performed 'What Makes You Beautiful'.

Taylor apparently mentioned to Justin Bieber that she thought Harry was hot. She said a quick 'Hello' to the boys, including Harry, backstage and then fanned herself afterwards, pretending she was overwhelmed by him. It was all good fun, although it did plant the seed that she fancied Harry, which would make future events more believable.

The First Lady, Michelle Obama, was the guest of honour and she presented Taylor with an award and chatted graciously with One Direction, who all thought she was lovely. Harry asked her if she and the president had trouble getting pizza delivered to the White House.

Perhaps as a cure for the hangover caused by the negativity that surrounded his relationship with Caroline Flack, Harry was cast as the lad about town when the *Up All Night* tour headed to Australasia. He was the one loudly cheering a wet t-shirt competition or photographed kissing a young, attractive blonde woman.

She turned out to be a Victoria's Secret model called Emma Ostilly, who was living in Auckland while on assignment in New Zealand. They had got on well apparently, when she appeared fleetingly in the video for 'Gotta Be You', which had been shot the previous year around Lake Placid, New York.

There was nothing in it, but that didn't stop speculation in the tabloids that they were an item. Harry was already learning that he only had to pass a woman in the street for them to be dating. More worryingly, Emma, who also modelled for Abercrombie & Fitch, was another victim of online abuse from One Direction fans and had to close her social media accounts.

Emma revealed she had been told not to say anything about Harry and she never has. She did not say why she had been told not to say anything or by whom. If it was all a publicity device aimed at demonstrating that Harry had moved on from Caroline Flack then it was not especially successful. As a rule of thumb, paparazzi tend not to just turn up – they are usually tipped off.

Emma flew back to the US and continued her modelling career. She remains best known, nine years later, for the Harry Styles kiss. Harry, meanwhile, continued the *Up All Night* tour in the US. The *Washington Post* captured the hysteria and the barrage of sound that greeted each of their 'puppy love anthems'. It reported that the noise was 'louder than an ambulance driving past a lawn mower in a thunderstorm'.

Returning to the UK in midsummer meant more work on the second album. Harry took time off with Liam and Niall to attend James Corden's wedding to Julia at Babington House near Frome, in Somerset. Ben Winston was best man and the couple's six-month-old son was the centre of attention.

Even James, a well-known celebrity, said he could not imagine what Harry's life was like. He had become so famous so quickly. James observed, 'The more normal people he has around, probably the better.'

He needed that normality when the previous year's fling with Lucy Horobin finally and belatedly made the Sunday papers. The year had been one of relentless triumph for Harry, but this was an unexpected downer. The negative publicity for him having assignations with another man's wife might have been much worse if they had been running at the same time as the Caroline Flack stories.

Lucy's marriage was all but over before she got together with Harry but that made no difference to the barrage of abuse and threats she received on Twitter – just as Caroline had done. She was called a 'paedophile', again, as Caroline had been. She posted, 'To clarify, I haven't said ANYTHING to any press, nor do I wish to. Thanks to those of you who have said kind words today. Xxx'

Lucy has been true to her word and has not spoken about Harry. Under the headline, 'Harry Styles slept with my wife', her soon-to-be ex-husband, a data analyst, stirred things further by declaring that he blamed Harry: 'He wasn't that into her but what happened between them ended our marriage.'

Clearly Harry was going to need something more than a kiss with a beautiful model to change the narrative about him. Five weeks later he was photographed holding hands with one of the most famous women in the world.

9

TAYLOR MADE

The first picture of Harry with Taylor Swift resembled a still from a rom-com movie. Of course it would be called *When Harry Met Taylor*. They looked a million dollars strolling through Central Park, New York, on a beautiful December afternoon. They were smiling easily, very much in step, wearing outfits to beat the chill that might have featured in a clothing catalogue. He had his hair pulled back under a favourite blue beanie; she sported a Fox sweater and maroon coat. They were the perfect couple and you could imagine the director yelling, 'Cut. It's a wrap. Let's go to the zoo everybody.'

A Sunday stroll in Central Park is like an announcement in *The Times*; formally letting everyone know you are an item. The photographs went all around the world. As is so often the case with well-chronicled romantic occasions, Harry and Taylor were not alone. They were with the One Direction stylist Lou Teasdale, singer Tom Atkin and their baby daughter Lux. Tom is the lead vocalist with Hull rock band The Paddingtons.

At the zoo, Taylor held Lux for a cuddle with Harry by her side as they watched the seals splashing around, while real mum and dad were out of shot watching on from the wings.

The walk in the park was just a week or so before Taylor's twenty-third birthday. Harry was still eighteen and had only been a star for a couple of years. Taylor, however, understood the pressures of being a teenager in the music business. She had released her first album, *Taylor Swift*, when she was sixteen and living in Nashville with her parents.

She wasn't from the home of country music, though. She had been brought up in Reading, Pennsylvania, with idyllic summers spent at a holiday home near the beach in New Jersey. Her parents had a business background but they encouraged their highly intelligent daughter to express herself and explore the pursuits she most enjoyed – acting and music.

The blot on her idyllic childhood was the bullying she suffered at school for being different. Unlike Harry, she was never very popular in class. Taylor's unhappiness with her peer group was one reason for her mum and dad's move to Nashville. Another was to enable their clearly talented fourteen-year-old daughter to pursue her musical ambitions.

Her first album won her recognition as a country artist and, more importantly, as a songwriter. Her second, *Fearless*, enabled her to cross over from country to mainstream. She won the Grammy Award for Album of the Year in 2010. At the age of twenty, she was the youngest ever recipient.

Intriguingly, bearing in mind Harry's future career path, she had also made her movie debut. She had a minor role in an ensemble romantic comedy and box office hit called *Valentine's Day*. She played a character called Felicia Miller and was involved in a subplot that revolved around kissing co-star Taylor Lautner, who had achieved heartthrob status through his role as vampire Jacob Black in the *Twilight* series of films.

The lip locks between them were so convincing that she was nominated in the Best Kiss category at the MTV Movie Awards. Predictably, the two Taylors were linked romantically for a month or two and were known as Taylor Squared, but it soon fizzled out. As she always seemed to do, she wrote a song about him – 'Back to December' – which featured on her *Speak Now* album.

Taylor spent a year performing the *Speak Now* world tour in support of her third album. Finishing in early 2012, she played 110 dates around the world before an estimated audience of 1.64 million. The figures were boggling, with tour receipts totalling more than $123 million. This was the first time Harry had been linked with someone even more famous than he was.

The UK had been surprisingly sluggish in its commercial appreciation of Taylor Swift, however. *Speak Now* had been a US number one and sold many millions there but in the UK, the album had been a bit of a flop, peaking at number six in the charts and selling less than 250,000 copies. The lead single from that album, 'Mine', only scraped to number thirty. Her school report for the UK read 'must do better'.

Much better was hoped for from her next album, *Red*, which she had spent most of the year writing and recording when her marathon tour had ended. One of her co-writers was another British star on the rise, Ed Sheeran. She had loved his song 'Lego House' that had been a hit in March. Unlike Harry and Ed, she wasn't a devotee of Lego bricks and didn't spend hours assembling tricky models. Harry bought his friend an Imperial Star Destroyer and the pair of them stayed up until 3am until it was complete.

Ed ended up co-writing outstanding tracks for both One Direction and Taylor: the sweet ballad 'Little Things' for *Take Me Home* and 'Everything Has Changed' for *Red*, which they wrote at her house in Beverly Hills, bouncing around on a trampoline in the garden. Across town Ed was with Harry for pizza day. Harry had a rare day off so he decided to buy lots of Domino's pizzas to hand out from his car to the homeless living in the Skid Row neighbourhood. Ed thought the take-aways ended up costing his friend between two and three thousand dollars. He said, 'People write about Harry in a negative way because of his love life but he does stuff like that a lot. He's a pretty genuine guy.'

'Little Things', the band's second UK number one, was on the set list when One Direction played Madison Square Garden in New York one day after the Central Park date. The concert in front of an 18,000-strong, predominantly female, teenage audience was 1D's most prestigious of the year. Ed came on stage when they performed 'Little Things' and sang a few lines with Harry. The concert was a triumph, with Dory Larrabee-Zayas in *Hollywood Life* noting how well the boys interacted with the fans, even jumping into the crowd at one point and posing for photos. Dory observed, 'I saw so many girls crying so hard, they looked like they were in pain, but they were tears of joy.' Taylor joined Harry at the after-show party where they were photographed and subsequently left together.

They were all back at Madison Square Garden a few days later for the annual Jingle Ball that featured eleven of the biggest acts of the year. During the week Harry had been photographed several times leaving the hotel in Tribeca where Taylor was said to be staying. Reports at the time suggested he looked pleased with himself, an unsubtle implication that he had been enjoying a night of passion with Taylor.

The set lists for the concert were an indication of where everyone was in their career at the time. One Direction opened the show and performed four numbers, including 'Little Things'. Ed sang just two, 'Lego House' and 'The A Team'. Taylor was top of the bill, sang six and closed the show, Ed joined her on stage for 'Everything has Changed'.

The *New York Times* reviewer, Ben Ratliff, said One Direction had 'bright smiles and uncoordinated body movements', whereas Taylor was the grown-up act of the night. Her set was 'several fathoms more elegant and sophisticated than anyone else's'. Ben added, 'The boss was in the house.' He did, however, repeat the speculation about a romantic link between Taylor and Harry. The fact that their connection was even mentioned demonstrated that the photo opportunities had done a good job.

The only one of Harry's close friends back in the UK to comment on the possible romance was the Radio 1 DJ Nick Grimshaw, with whom he used to speak frequently on the phone. Nick revealed, 'Harry really likes Taylor. At first I wasn't sure if the relationship was a real one but I talk to him a lot and it seems to be that she is the one – for now, anyway.'

Harry and Taylor barely had time to catch their breath before they were bound for London on her private jet. One Direction was appearing at London's equivalent Jingle Ball at the O2. And then they were at Manchester Central Arena as guests for the final of that year's *The X Factor*, when they performed 'Kiss You', another track from *Take Me Home*.

There would be plenty more photographs, especially when Harry took Taylor to Cheshire, where they wandered around Tesco in Manchester Road, Northwich – as superstars do. Harry bought some hair gel while excited shoppers, scarcely believing their eyes, watched as Taylor wandered up and down the fresh vegetable aisle.

The supermarket was one stop on a mini-break that included a trip with Harry's mum over to Bowness-on-Windermere, although it's a one-hundred-mile trek from her home, so not exactly down the road. Taylor joined in to feed the pigeons and swans and bought half of the gift store when they went to visit Beatrix Potter's house, Hill Top. Taylor loved the Lake District and would subsequently write a track called 'The Lakes' in its honour.

Harry and Taylor, who the media had named 'Haylor', also travelled to The Rising Sun pub in the Peak District, ten miles from his sister Gemma's university in Sheffield. Taylor nibbled some black pudding for the first time, although she was apprehensive when told the staple ingredient was pig's blood. For her twenty-third birthday, Harry gave her twenty-three custom-made cupcakes from a speciality shop in Warrington. He did not place the order himself, though. For good measure, he gave her two handbags, a pair of antique earrings and a photo frame containing a black and white picture of a famous pop star – himself, of course. For a man as discreet as Harry about relationships that matter, there was a surprisingly large amount of information about this one in the public domain.

If success is measured in column inches, then this whirl-wind mini-break had been a triumph. There was more to come. This time Harry was the one visiting home territory when he accompanied Taylor to Nashville, where he met her family. Back in Los Angeles, she joined him on some tattoo trips to the Shamrock Social Club, although she chose not to have one done at the same time.

He was having his striking galleon tattoo inked onto his left arm, again by Freddy Negrete. Harry didn't choose the design until he arrived at the salon and flipped through a book of old paintings of ships. He told Freddy that he wanted something to represent sailing home: 'We're always on the road but my heart is at home and I want a ship.'

The image, which many thought resembled Nelson's flag-ship HMS *Victory*, was a complicated tattoo that took several visits. Freddy was very happy with the results. He thought that Harry and Taylor seemed more like friends than two young people in love. He later said, 'There wasn't a sparkle in Harry's eye. They were kind and respectful to each other but didn't have stars in their eyes.'

The tattoo is on his left arm placed underneath his sister Gemma's name in Hebrew, a gesture acknowledging his inter-est in what Ben had told him about his Jewish culture back in Hampstead Garden Suburb. Harry had carefully written out the translation, realising that this was not something to get wrong.

Harry and Taylor didn't spend Christmas together – she was on a promotional trip to Australia and he was in Cheshire again. Naturally his family had asked him what present he wanted. He confided, 'I asked for socks and pants because if you're out on the road, you always run out.' His mum gave him a big beautifully wrapped box that wasn't full of underwear. When he finished carefully removing all the sparkly paper he discovered the small gift for the teenager who has everything – a belly button brush. Harry loved it.

He and Taylor did manage a New Year break in the British Virgin Islands but she left early amid reports of an 'almighty row'. He took a boat over to Necker at the invitation of the island's owner, Richard Branson, where he swam, sunbathed and was sociable. Then he flew back to Heathrow. Haylor was over.

During their briefest of time together, both *Red* and *Take Me Home* topped the *Billboard* album charts in the US. That was particularly significant for One Direction because it meant that they were the first British act to have their first two albums debut at the top of the US charts. Were Harry and Taylor ever going to be the next superstar couple following in the golden footsteps of Beyoncé and Jay-Z, Kim Kardashian and Kanye West or, looking further back, Justin Timberlake and Britney Spears?

The cynical answer is not a chance. But reflecting on that famous walk in Central Park, Harry said, 'Relationships are hard at any age. And adding in that you don't really understand exactly how it works when you're eighteen, trying to navigate all that stuff didn't make it easier. I mean, you're a little bit awkward to begin with. You're on a date with someone you really like. It should be that simple, right? It was a learning experience for sure. But at the heart of it – I just wanted it to be a normal date.'

He was still only eighteen and it seemed much of his life was a 'learning experience'. He surrounded himself with older friends who coloured the way he looked at the world. Taylor may have been only five or so years older but she was an enlightened young woman of the world. In the coming years both she and Harry would become strong supporters of the LGBTQ+ community and would have to answer intrusive questions about their own sexuality.

Harry's friendship with Nick Grimshaw, for instance, was a classic case of 'He's gay, therefore you must be too.' Nick was one of Harry's 'Thirtysomething' inner circle who was great fun on a night out or just an afternoon playing Frisbee in the park. 'Grimmy', as he is called by many, was once memorably described as possessing 'the air of a gossipy older brother with access to the best parties'. Harry was one of many who enjoyed his vivacious company.

Nick Grimshaw grew up in Oldham, just north of Manchester and wasn't officially 'out' until 2012. He spoke openly about his sexuality the same month that he was announced as the new host of the Breakfast Show on Radio 1, taking over from Chris Moyles – perhaps diffusing any lurid tabloid headlines before they were written.

Newspapers still tend to treat someone's sexuality as big news. Back in the eighties, George Michael was forever being pestered about it. He refused to confirm or deny the inevitable question about the gay rumours that seemed to slip into every interview. For a while, he liked the ambiguity, claiming that sort of thing had done no harm to the careers of David Bowie or Mick Jagger – two of the artists Harry greatly admired. George said, 'I don't think anyone should have to answer a "gay or straight" question.' But he kept being asked.

One of the triggers for the rumours that Harry and Nick were romantically involved appeared to be Harry's liking for floral shirts. During the coming months, they both responded to gossip that they were dating. Nick told *Now* magazine about their friendship: 'It seems totally normal to me; a DJ being mates with a pop star.'

Harry even had to respond to a direct question from *GQ* magazine. He answered simply, 'No, we're not dating. We're just friends.'

10

17 BLACK

———

Goodness knows how Harry and Nick made it to the Radio 1 studio for the DJ's breakfast show. They had literally been 'up all night' after the 2013 BRIT Awards the evening before. At least Nick had changed his shirt. Harry was still wearing the same smart suit that was looking a little bit more crumpled than it had done on the red carpet.

They had done the rounds of the after-parties, enjoying Champagne and Belvedere cocktails at the Warner Music Group event at the Savoy Hotel before going on to the Sony thrash at the Arts Club in Mayfair. The night was still young – maybe 4.30ish – when they piled into taxis with friends including the actress Jaime Winstone to continue the festivities at Nick's flat in Primrose Hill. Just before 6am they were on their way to BBC Broadcasting House in Portland Place.

Harry teased Nick on air, asking innocently: 'Grimmy, how many hours' sleep have you had since yesterday?' He certainly seemed in better shape than his older friend. Lily Allen tweeted, '@grimmers you sound hammered still.'

Harry didn't stick around long, leaving Nick to battle through, apologise for being unusually quiet on the show and admit he was in a 'pretty fragile state'. Then it was home for a 'very long sleep'.

The one party the pair had avoided was held by the Universal Music Group at Soho House. Taylor Swift was there. Several close friends were also present, including Ben Winston and James Corden, the consummate professional, who was completely at ease with Taylor when they messed around with some DJing.

James had earlier again been the host at the main event when both Taylor and One Direction had performed. Taylor sang 'I Knew You Were Trouble', which conveniently hinted she was referring to Harry, even though she had written and released it before they had taken their walk in Central Park.

When asked by the *Sunday Times* if it was difficult to perform the song on the night, she said, 'Well, it's not hard to access that emotion when the person the song is directed at is standing by the side of the stage watching.' There was, it seemed, still mileage to be had in the previous month's break-up, so it wouldn't have worked as well if they had been smiling and sharing a joke or two that evening.

They had avoided each other at rehearsal and on the night itself when One Direction followed her on to perform their Comic Relief single 'One Way or Another (Teenage Kicks)'. Three days later it entered the UK chart at number one. Taylor's single wasn't doing too badly either, going back up to number six. *Red* would finally become her first UK number one album in May.

One Direction was a big winner on the night, claiming the Global Success Award, recognising the group's impact around the world. The Damien Hirst-designed statuette was presented to them by Robbie Williams, two years and two months after he had shepherded them through the final of *The X Factor*.

Comic Relief was an enormous charity event and in 2013 raised more than £100 million. One Direction spent two days in Accra, the capital of Ghana, making a series of video diaries highlighting poverty and the need for improved medical facilities. Harry was seen crying in a hospital ward at the plight of a baby boy stricken with malaria: 'If you get involved in it and you don't cry, then you're superhuman.'

Harry explained how he felt about the reality of everyday life in a poor country and how he was unprepared for the hardship he witnessed firsthand: 'We thought we knew what it's like. But when you're there and you get the smells, your eyes hurt from the smoke, you cough, you're feeling it all. It's crazy how quick you get connections with children and the people who live there. You feel upset leaving them and saying goodbye to them.'

Away from the highly publicised charity life of One Direction, Harry was supporting the endeavours of his mum. Anne was creating her own future promoting charities that mattered to her and raising money for them. She would never have to worry about money for herself because her son was a multi-millionaire. But she didn't want him to just write out a cheque for her latest cause – where was the sense of achievement in that?

Instead, she decided to climb Mount Kilimanjaro in Tanzania for a charity she backed called Believe in Magic, which helped seriously and terminally ill children. She undertook her adventure with four friends, including Vicky Sherlock, the mother of Ashley Sherlock, one of Harry's best friends from Holmes Chapel Comprehensive. Robin Twist boosted the fundraising by organising a sponsored chest wax.

The expedition raised nearly £28,000. Afterwards Harry tweeted, 'Very proud of my mum today, she is on her way home after reaching the top of Mount Kilimanjaro.' Subsequently, Believe in Magic was mired in allegations of financial irregularity and, after an inquiry, was removed from the charity register in 2020.

Fortunately, the controversy did not deter Anne's philanthropic nature and she continued to promote the charities she cared about, especially Parkinson's UK. Her father – and Harry's beloved grandfather – Brian had been diagnosed with the disease in his early seventies.

A week after Comic Relief, Harry ensured that Brian, then aged seventy-seven, was his personal guest of honour when One Direction played the O2 arena for the first time. Anne, Robin and Gemma were also there to make sure Brian was looked after during the concert. Before he went on stage, Harry went up to chat to his granddad. 'He hasn't changed at all,' said Brian. 'He always has a smile on his face and is very loving and caring. I don't think of him as this well-known pop star.'

Everyone was worried that Brian would find the noise of the fans overwhelming, but he was a member of an older generation who remembered Beatlemania and he took it in his stride. He observed, 'The girls were screaming so loud – it was deafening, but I would really like to go again.'

The extended Styles family were very close and remained so despite the pressure of fame. Harry slipped quietly into a hospital in Peterborough to visit another elderly member who had fallen ill. His grandmother Beryl, mother of Des and known affectionately as Nanny Styles, was unwell. It made her nurses' day to discover Harry Styles sitting by her bedside. Sadly, Nanny died the following year after a long illness when Harry was on tour in the US, but he flew straight over. The newspapers concentrated on what he was wearing when he arrived at Heathrow.

A happier family occasion was the wedding of Robin and Anne. They seemed to have been engaged for years before they married quietly at the upmarket Pecks restaurant in Congleton. The wedding was arranged for the break in the *Take Me Home* tour between the last gig on the European leg in Lisbon and the first concert across the Atlantic in Mexico. The occasion was kept so secret that the fifty guests weren't told of the location until the last minute so that the ceremony wouldn't be hijacked by over-enthusiastic Directioners. A decoy bus with fake wedding guests on board was even sent to Doncaster racecourse eighty miles away to fool any fans loitering in the area.

Harry shared best man duties with his new elder step-brother, Mike Twist, who was Robin's son from a previous marriage. This was Anne's big day and the bride was the centre of attention in an exquisite, traditional, full-length white gown, trimmed with lace. The best men and the groom wore matching dark suits.

The wedding illustrated Harry and his family's ongoing attitude towards keeping their private lives private. They would post a tweet or two and the odd photograph but there was never any question of a photographer from *Hello!* or another glossy magazine turning such happy events into a media circus.

That may explain what happened to his close friendship with his high-school friend, bakery pal and fellow band member in White Eskimo, Nick Clough. He gave an interview to a Sunday newspaper which was flagged as revealing 'all about the beer, the band, the girls, the tattoos ...'

The revelations seemed harmless enough and rather sweet. He recalled driving Harry's Audi R8, which he loved: 'I'm more jealous of the cars than anything.' He did mention Caroline Flack and Taylor Swift briefly but the only off-colour anecdote involved Harry getting 'his k★★b out' and pressing it against the window of one of his friends' mum's car. No one was offended, recalled Nick.

The article was accompanied by a series of never-before-seen photographs of Harry as a teenager at school and playing with White Eskimo. They haven't been seen again. The words and pictures appeared a few weeks before the wedding. Nick wasn't invited. In fact, he hasn't spoken a word to Harry since the newspaper piece. He said simply: 'Unfortunately my article with the *Sunday Mirror* cost me my friendship with Harry.'

Nick is not alone in no longer being in contact with Harry. Will Sweeny, for instance, hasn't spoken to Harry since those days. Felicity Skinner last spoke to him the week before Judges' Houses on *The X Factor*.

Ed Sheeran was very much one of Harry's new friends who understood the line between privacy and public image where performers were concerned. Ed has never said a word about

Harry and Taylor's relationship despite spending time with both of them. He would meet up with Harry when his touring schedule with the latter allowed. He was drinking with him one night when they decided to get a tattoo together.

The following day Ed called Kevin Paul, his favourite tattoo artist in London, and asked him to meet them at one of Harry's houses the next Sunday morning. Kevin recalled, 'Harry and Ed had been out the night before, got pissed and started talking about their favourite childhood shows and Pingu was both of their favourite, which is why they both decided to get them.'

Ed opted for an illustration of the actual naughty penguin while Harry went for a more obvious PINGU lettering on his left bicep. Harry also wanted a tattoo of 17 Black, which became one of his best-known ones. Everyone assumed that it was a reference to James Bond's lucky bet in the 1971 film *Diamonds Are Forever*.

Harry loved roulette but he was not as successful playing 17 Black as Sean Connery had been in the film; far from it. He had first lost heavily when One Direction went to a casino in Perth, Western Australia, during their *Up All Night* tour. They all did except Niall, who won £100 and then stopped and watched the others keep digging. He said, 'Let's just say a lot of money was lost. A lot. When management found out, we got a serious dressing down.'

Harry lost on 17 Black so his new tattoo, high on the left side of his chest, was a reminder of that or perhaps heralding a change of luck. It didn't work. He wandered into the VIP area of the casino in Perth during their *Take Me Home* tour and had another unsuccessful night with his 'lucky' number.

At least the tattoo looked good, which is more than could be said for the one Ed inked on Harry's left forearm. Kevin set up the machine for them and Ed carefully drew a padlock, although Harry was later heard to remark that he thought it looked more like a handbag. Fortunately for Ed, they ran out of time before Harry was able to get his revenge.

Perhaps his best-known tattoo was already in place – a large butterfly across the middle of his chest. This time he went to Liam Sparkes at Old Habits Tattoo in Hackney, another of his favourite parlours. You couldn't miss the result. A butterfly is a popular symbol, representing the transformation of life from child to adult. Liam also pointed to the film *Papillon* as being an inspiration. In the 1973 version Steve McQueen plays Henri Charrière, a safecracker named Papillon because of the giant butterfly tattooed on his chest.

Harry's butterfly stood out proudly below a tattoo of two swallows facing each other. He explained that he particularly liked the old-fashioned type of tattoo that sailors would traditionally have: 'They symbolise travelling and we travel a lot.'

The aptly named *Take Me Home* tour was a marathon and a reminder that One Direction was a successful business and the five members were the majority shareholders. They performed 123 shows across the globe, including concerts in the US, Japan, Australia and six nights at the O2. More than 300,000 tickets were sold for the UK and Ireland leg in one day while 108,000 fans screamed at them at the Fara Sol stadium in Mexico City.

The public face of the band was that they were just five lads having fun – but the reality was very different. Andy Greene, an associate editor with *Rolling Stone* magazine, commented,

'It's insane; they're working them like dogs and printing money right now.' The tour generated well over $100 million.

Simon Cowell had already said that he did not want to introduce rules for the boys as if they were still at school, not least because they would just break them. He observed, 'They're good-looking guys and they all like girls.'

In practice, it was not a sex free-for-all. Lou Teasdale, who was responsible for make-up and style on all the tours since the *X Factor* days, revealed that sex with the band was strictly off limits. It was a no-tolerance policy. She explained, 'You can't sleep with them. It's kind of important if you want to keep your job.'

Occasionally a member of staff, perhaps a newcomer, crossed that line and they were swiftly shown the door. They might have thought it was true love but it wasn't. The boys and those looking after them did not want to provoke an embarrassing incident if a new girlfriend was on the scene.

In any case, there wasn't much time for anything extra-curricular. As well as performing, travelling between gigs on a tour bus or plane and checking into soulless hotels, they were busy recording their third album, literally on the road.

Hotel rooms were doubling as makeshift recording studios with beds flipped up against the wall. They would work on a new song for twenty minutes before having to leave for the show, then perform for a couple of hours, come back and put in some more time before bed. The recording was their winding up and winding down. The bonus from a musical point of view was that the boys were still in the zone. The demo vocal recorded in a hotel after midnight was often better than the version in a million-dollar studio.

Two LA-based writers and producers, Julian Bunetta and John Ryan, were largely responsible for steering One Direction's musical progress to the next stage. They had worked for Syco on *X Factor USA* and on *Take Me Home* and collaborated on more than half of the tracks on the new album.

Both Savan Kotecha and Carl Falk had young families, so it was left to Julian and John to step up and travel around the world, although most of the groundwork for what would become *Midnight Memories* was prepared in London. They both realised that the members of One Direction were moving forward as a band. Julian explained, 'They needed to grow up or they were going to go away – and they wanted to grow up.'

All five of One Direction had input into the writing of their third album, some more than others. Louis, for instance, had a credit on nine of the songs. Harry featured on only four but, more interestingly, he was the sole band member on two of the tracks, 'Happily' and 'Something Great', suggesting he was beginning to find his own songwriting identity. 'Something Great' was co-written with Gary Lightbody, the lead singer with Snow Patrol, and that band's long-standing producer, Jacknife Lee. In the very small world of the music premiership, they had collaborated with Taylor Swift on *Red*. Gary was also great mates with Ed Sheeran, who had toured the US supporting his band the previous year.

Harry was also more prominent in the lead singles from the album, 'Best Song Ever' and 'Story of my Life'. He was centre stage for both videos that were directed by his landlord, Ben Winston.

The 'Story of my Life' was a painstakingly put-together work of art, drawing on collections of old childhood photographs. Ben explained his use of the family album snaps: 'You are still from the same place. That is the story of their life.' The mums were enlisted as well and Anne couldn't stop smiling next to Harry singing away.

Ben was one of the producers of *One Direction: This Is Us*. Leicester Square had to be sealed off for the evening when a football-stadium-size crowd of teenage girls descended on central London, many camping out overnight to ensure their place at the front of the queue. A week later the same thing happened at the New York premiere at the Ziegfeld Theatre on West 54th Street in midtown Manhattan. The area was brought to a standstill.

Each fan seemed to have their favourite, although there did seem to be a lot of Harry in evidence. His name was painted on foreheads, Harry dolls and masks were waved and t-shirts proclaimed: 'Harry You Wanna Marry Me?'

The authorised 3D film was directed by Morgan Spurlock, who had sprung to prominence for his documentary *Super Size Me* about his existence on a diet of McDonald's food (and would later achieve notoriety after confessing to sexual misconduct). The final movie managed to keep everyone happy. The *New York Times* commented, 'The film catches the singers at their most adorable: adjusting to fame, marvelling at the devotion of the fans, and often taking off their shirts.'

The newspaper also observed that 'there is little indication of romance, and absolutely no alcohol, cigarettes, drugs or sex'. This was a documentary that reflected the enthusiasm and exuberance of five boys on a yellow brick road to adulthood. Ben, who had travelled with them remarked that the band was determined 'to squeeze every bit of fun and joy' out of their journey.

Obviously the target audience was their fans, the Directioners, the already converted who needed no persuading to go and see the film. Their devotion turned into box-office gold. *One Direction: This Is Us* earned more than $67 million dollars worldwide on a budget of $10 million. The DVD alone sold 270,000 copies within three days.

Ben neatly defined One Direction's philosophy on what was happening to them: 'We will always be part of the biggest part of each other's lives.'

1D was still very much part of Harry's life but as he prepared to leave his teenage years behind, there were already signs that the twenty-something man would be moving away from being just another member of a boy band.

11

THE ARCHITECTURE
OF HAPPINESS

———————

When Harry met the philosopher Alain de Botton, one of the leading lights of London intelligentsia, they talked easily of Aristotle, Plato, love and beauty. Harry was never tongue-tied at parties. His life experiences and natural inquisitiveness made him an ideal guest. He wasn't fazed by money, reputation or intelligence.

A first, casual chat with Alain was not a eureka moment for Harry, but it would prove to be an indication of a man on a thoughtful and enlightened path. Alain was impressed: 'Reports of the death of culture in the young are much exaggerated: Harry is a real enthusiast of Greek philosophy.'

Alain was born in Switzerland, the son of the prominent international financier, multi-millionaire and art collector, Gilbert de Botton. He moved to England as a schoolboy, attending Harrow and then Cambridge before obtaining a master's degree in philosophy at King's College London.

He became well known first as a writer of both fiction and non-fiction before reaching a wider audience through broadcasting, lectures and workshops. His meeting with Harry prompted him to reach out to the pop world as a means of communicating important ideas to the next generation.

He urged pop stars to suggest to their fans that they should read the classical philosophers. He expanded on the thought: 'My plan is to shut the Arts Council and get people such as Harry Styles to go on television and recommend to everyone they read Proust and Hegel, which would achieve more in five minutes than the Arts Council achieves year in, year out.

'David Beckham could do Aristotle and Plato ... and in an ideal world Harry Styles would be teaching his ten million Twitter followers a little more about Greek philosophy.'

To illustrate Alain's point, Harry responded by immediately tweeting a sentence from Wikipedia, 'Socrates, born in Athens in the 5th century BC, marks a watershed in Ancient Greek philosophy.' The post would be retweeted 56,000 times and liked by 47,000 users.

Newspaper columnists saw this exchange as an open goal to poke fun at Alain and Harry's expense. Sam Leith wrote in the *Guardian*: 'We are accustomed to thinking of him as an intellectual lightweight, a Twitter-addicted, sex-obsessed celebrity socialite quite incapable of holding his end up in a conversation about philosophy with Harry Styles.'

Alain, then forty-three, took it all in good part because he genuinely liked Harry and appreciated that he was an 'intelligent chap'. He said, 'It's important to try and bridge this gap between popular culture and what people see as highbrow. Hopefully, this will be the start of Harry engaging with more philosophy.'

It was. Quietly and with no fuss, Harry would stay in contact with Alain, reading his books, listening to his podcast,

The True Hard Work of Love and Relationships, and even discreetly attending his workshops. He has been an admirer ever since their first meeting. In his now celebrated 2020 *Vogue* cover story, Harry paid tribute to the philosopher: 'I just think he's brilliant. I saw him give a talk about the keys to happiness, and how one of the keys is living among friends, and how real friendship stems from being vulnerable with someone.'

Living with friends as a key to happiness helps to explain Harry's enjoyment of living in Ben and Meredith Winston's house. He was not just being eccentric, after all, and this would not be the last time that he chose a similar living arrangement. *The Architecture of Happiness* (2006) was one of the books written by Alain that Harry kept on his bookshelves. Again, it highlighted the importance of environment in well-being.

Harry would later mix the world of fashion with that of philosophy when he designed a hoodie that displayed three pictures of Alain across the front. He wore it to be interviewed by *Vogue*, the fashion bible. By this time, 2020, anything Harry wore was going to become a talking point.

That was not the case in the early days of One Direction but big-name brands identified him as the best member of the group to target. One of the true ironies of being so successful in the world of celebrity is being able to afford anything you want but never having to buy a thing because you receive it all for free. He could have opened his own designer-label clothing store with the amount of merchandise he was sent. It was always worth a punt to send him something just in case it took his fancy. If he was photographed wearing a particular t-shirt, for instance, it would be advertising gold.

Harry's bedroom resembled a stroll round the menswear department of Selfridges – Ray-Bans, Adidas and Nike trainers and Ralph Lauren polo shirts were just some of the brands competing for his attention. He always stood out as the classiest dresser in One Direction.

Harry spent most of 2013 touring but had a month off between *Take Me Home* shows in Los Angeles in mid-August and the resumption in Adelaide in late September, so he had the chance to ditch the band and attend various events at that year's London Fashion Week. He clearly loved being involved. He was in good spirits, laughing and joking in the front row next to Nick Grimshaw, Kelly Osbourne and Nicola Roberts at Henry Holland's runway show at Somerset House.

Harry was a late arrival but immediately became the centre of attention for the photographers. He chose to wear a label-free, plain white t-shirt and jeans, a neat gesture to avoid favouritism. Afterwards, he told *E! News* that he liked the hats.

After House of Hutton, it was over to Kensington Gardens for the Burberry Prorsum Show, where he was sat between two very glamorous blondes, Suki Waterhouse and Sienna Miller. The assembled media, however, were more interested in his reaction to watching supermodel Cara Delevingne on the runway. One reporter set a trap for him by asking innocently, 'Are you looking forward to seeing your girl Cara walk down the runway?' Harry responded, sharply: 'She's not my girl. I know what you're doing.'

Harry went backstage after the show to congratulate Cara and chat. He posed for pictures with her but had donned a black balaclava with the letters BS scrawled in white across the top – an abbreviation for bullshit – which may or may not have been aimed at photographers intruding on this occasion. They both well knew that these balaclava pictures could not be dragged out year after year as enduring proof of their relationship.

The rumours about Cara and Harry had been keeping the gossip pages interested for months. They seemed intent on never being photographed together – no walks in Central Park – although they were captured on camera by a member of the audience at the Prince of Wales Theatre enjoying the hit musical *The Book of Mormon*, a few days before London Fashion Week. Harry was clearly visible but the only way celebrity sleuths could deduce that Cara was the blonde woman sitting next to him in the dress circle was by the lion tattoo on her finger.

They were said to have been dating secretly for years and the most likely confirmation of that is that they were not 'spotted' together. Magazines and online diaries would cheat by running full-length pictures of them side by side, hoping that readers would not realise they were snapped on completely different occasions and they weren't actually *together* when the photographs were taken.

Cara, twenty, had quickly become fashion royalty, winning Model of the Year at the 2012 British Fashion Awards. She was brought up in the higher echelons of London society, but her early life was far from an upper-class glide. Her father, Charles Delevingne, is a property developer and her socialite mother, Pandora, is the daughter of the late Sir Jocelyn Stevens, a publishing magnate, and Jane Sheffield, lady-in-waiting to Princess Margaret. Pandora has been frank about her struggles with heroin addiction and a bipolar diagnosis. Cara's elder sister and fellow supermodel, Poppy Delevingne, tried to shelter her younger sibling from the worst of it by letting her sleep in her bed for years. Even so, Cara has admitted to suffering from a deep depression at the age of fifteen.

With the benefit of hindsight it's easy to identify the connection between Cara and Harry. They are kindred spirits both on their career paths and their willingness to embrace non-toxic criteria in their lives – and neither liked society's need to put a label on everything. Cara Delevingne was not 'Harry's girl' and he hated being linked to every girl who stood next to him.

Over the years she has patiently explained that she is not 'gay', she is sexually fluid, a young woman who enjoys relations with men and women. She observed, 'Once I spoke about my sexual fluidity, people were like, "So you're gay." And I'm like, "No I'm not gay."' She told *Glamour* magazine, 'I am very happy how sexuality has become easier and freer to talk about, especially for kids.'

More recently, in 2020, Cara, now a Hollywood fixture, was on the front cover of *Variety* magazine's Pride issue, in which she described herself as 'pansexual' – attracted to all genders. *Variety* observed that she is one of Hollywood's most visible queer actors.

Harry has had to bat away potentially explosive questions about his sexuality. His response to being asked if he was bisexual was, 'Bisexual? Me? I don't think so. I'm pretty sure I'm not.'

Cara and Harry were very much part of the same 'fashionable' London circle back in 2013, which included Poppy, Nick Grimshaw, Rita Ora, Pixie Geldof, Kelly Osbourne,

Jack Guinness and the uber-stylish Alexa Chung. Harry was with everyone for Alexa's thirtieth birthday party in November at the Edition Hotel in Soho and happily posed for pictures that ended up on Instagram.

Alexa, who was ten years older than Harry, loved his company. She enthused that he was amazing and radiated a magnetic quality: 'If he looks at you, it's like staring into the face of a lighthouse. I don't know what it is about that boy, he's just incredibly charming.'

Harry was readily accepted into this world. He even gate-crashed Poppy's hen party in early December at the Groucho Club, in Soho, when he donned a long blonde wig, pretending to be a member of former teen favourites Hanson. He danced around to the band's 1997 number one 'MMMBop', ending up sitting in the bride-to-be's lap.

Some commentators hinted that a member of a teenage boy band was perhaps not high end enough to mix in such exalted fashion circles, but that was proven to be nonsense two days later when Harry became the first man to win the British Style Award at the British Fashion Awards, the fashion equivalent of the BRITs or the BAFTAs. Alison Jane Reid observed, 'It's a big deal within the fashion industry.'

While the award, backed by Vodaphone, was voted for by the public, the fact that Harry was nominated in the first place demonstrated that he was a fully accepted face of fashion and not just a celebrity pop star brightening the front rows of runway shows or looking good with a supermodel on his arm. He was described as 'embodying the spirit of London' and as 'an international ambassador for London as a leading creative fashion capital'.

The nominations for his year included David Beckham, Kate Moss, Kate Middleton and, coincidentally, Cara Delevingne. For once the list did not include Alexa, who had won for the previous three years. This time she had to make do with co-presenting the award with the writer and former model Jack Guinness at the London Coliseum.

Harry was elegantly dressed in a Saint Laurent suit by Hedi Slimane. Suits suited Harry. Hedi Slimane, the creative director first at Dior and then at YSL, is responsible for what Alison Jane describes as 'the skinny silhouette in menswear since 2000'. He was heavily influenced by the music scene and youth culture that Harry, for one, represented.

The style winner kept his acceptance speech very short: 'Thank you for voting; this is very very kind. Thank you for having me here. I really appreciate it. Thank you.' The next day, Harry's success was the only fashion story in town.

More and more it was becoming clear that Harry would be the centre of attention wherever he went. The best he could hope for was to keep quiet until after the event. That was the strategy with his big sister's graduation at Sheffield Hallam University.

He was sat next to his mum and couldn't have looked any more delighted when Gemma went on stage to receive her degree from Professor Robert Winston, Ben's dad, who was chancellor of the university. She had achieved First Class Honours and Qualified Teacher Status in Science Education.

Afterwards, Harry posed for a picture with Gemma that he posted on Instagram with the short message: 'My sister graduated today. She's all clever and that.' And that was all he had to say – it wasn't about him and it wasn't his day. The university followed up by posting a couple of photographs on Twitter with the caption: 'A special guest attended today's graduation ceremony to see his sister collect her degree. Welcome @Harry_Styles.'

Privately, however, Harry was receiving some very unwelcome attention. He couldn't, it seemed, move without hearing the click of more than one paparazzi camera. It was time to take action. Quietly, he instructed David Sherborne, one of the most celebrated lawyers in the country, to institute legal proceedings on his behalf.

David was the go-to lawyer for A-list litigants, having represented Princess Diana, Michael Douglas, Sienna Miller, Kate Moss and many more. At the Leveson Inquiry into the British press he represented 'core participants' including the McCanns, J.K. Rowling and Hugh Grant.

In more recent times he has been instructed by Meghan Markle and Johnny Depp.

On Harry's behalf, he won a court order against a group of paparazzi. The unnamed photographers were ordered by Mrs Justice Nicola Davies to stop pursuing Harry by car or motorcycle, placing him under surveillance or loitering within fifty metres of his place of residence in order to monitor his movements.

Harry was mindful of not appearing precious and unaccommodating to his loyal fans. David told the court: 'This is not a privacy injunction. Mr Styles is not trying to prevent fans approaching him in the street and taking photos. He remains happy to do that as he always has. Rather, it is the method or tactics which have been used by a certain type of photographer.'

This was a significant victory for Harry, although he was not in court and made no comment about the case. He had hated the way Caroline Flack couldn't even open her front door when she was in a relationship with him. He was determined to put a stop to it as far as he was concerned.

Professionally, things could hardly have been going better. *Midnight Memories* had been released towards the end of November and was already astonishingly successful. One Direction became the first act to debut at number one on the US *Billboard* chart with its first three albums. In the UK, it was the fastest-selling album of 2013, clocking up sales in the first week of release of 237,000.

The demand was exceptional everywhere and by the end of year *Midnight Memories* was the best-selling album in the world, with sales of four million. The critics generally seemed on board with the slightly different, rockier sound – more guitar throwback than Euro pop synthesisers. *USA Today*'s Brian Mansfield was encouraging: 'The best songs, such as the current single, "Story of My Life," suggest the group's finest memories may still lie ahead.' Alison Stewart in the *Washington Post* noted, 'The songs are expertly made, impressively (sometimes very impressively) sung, nominally more adult and in every way quite decent, which is all they need to be.'

Tongue-in-cheek, Alison also wondered, 'Who might be the first to unwisely go solo? To be hospitalised for "exhaustion"? Which one is Justin Timberlake?'

One Direction's first stadium tour had been announced for 2014. They would be spending six months on the road performing at the largest venues throughout the world. How could they possibly keep up this pace?

12

KEEPING UP
WITH HARRY

Behind the scenes progress was being quietly made about Harry's future. He was proving to be very popular in important showbusiness circles in Los Angeles. He fitted in. He was charming, good company and very discreet. He was always the one in One Direction.

A very significant development had occurred without fanfare before One Direction had even released a record. Back in August 2011, Simon Cowell's Syco Entertainment had formed a partnership with Front Line Management, the largest management company in the world.

The deal was for Front Line to manage the winners of the American version of *The X Factor*, which was about to launch in the US. It was an arrangement totally separate from the UK where contestants, including 1D, were handled by Modest Management.

The chairman and CEO of Front Line was Irving Azoff, arguably the most influential man in the music business. He was also in charge at Ticketmaster and was executive chairman of Live Nation Entertainment. In 2012 he topped *Billboard's*

Power 100, recognising him as the most powerful man in the industry. He was the ultimate behind-the-scenes player.

Since he started as a manager in the 1970s he had a long association with some of the biggest names in pop and rock, including the Eagles and Fleetwood Mac, two of Harry's favourites growing up.

His son Jeffrey was following in his father's footsteps, learning the business as a manager at Front Line with ambitions to strike out on his own at some point. His wife Shelli has been the best friend of reality matriarch Kris Jenner for more than thirty years; his daughter Allison Statter went to school with Kim Kardashian and is her oldest and dearest friend – one who shuns the limelight.

Harry stepped easily into this world. A social meeting of music folk in Los Angeles quickly led to Harry becoming part of the Azoff/Kardashian/Jenner circle. He and Jeffrey, who was eight years older, hit it off straight away. This was more than a possible professional interest somewhere in the future. Harry was soon practically part of the family and socialised with the Azoff friends, including the Kardashians and Jenners.

The nearest in age to Harry was Kendall Jenner, who was just a year his junior. The world knew of their friendship when they were photographed in November 2013 after having dinner at the renowned celebrity haunt Craig's in Melrose Avenue. The restaurant was a favourite of the Azoff and Kardashian clans.

This is not the place to go for a quiet meal if you are as well known as these two. It's not that you are going to be photographed dribbling spaghetti sauce down your chin. The hazard is when you arrive and leave as there is always the chance of paparazzi hanging around hoping to catch sight of Kim Kardashian looking fabulous.

Sure enough, Kendall and Harry were snapped leaving in his black Range Rover Sport. Kendall was in the passenger seat checking messages on her mobile phone. Harry was driving and looking straight ahead. Neither of them was smiling for the cameras. In fact, the opposite was true. They looked as if they were gritting their teeth in frustration at not even being allowed to grab some food without having their picture taken. Harry had already made it obvious through his High Court action that he hated this sort of intrusion.

The resulting photographs could scarcely have been less interesting but they still made the papers all around the world and became a hot topic on social media. Kendall was quickly sick of it – she tweeted, 'Enough with the rumours! I'm single, people.' Harry was even asked if they were dating on national television. He answered Piers Morgan's question, 'I mean, we went out for dinner, but no, I guess.'

The next night he was back at Craig's but this time he was meeting Jeffrey Azoff and they definitely weren't dating. He would dine there many times over the years but almost always as a guest of the Azoffs, the Kardashians or the Jenners – or all three.

At least Kendall was a more believable romance than some of his alleged flings. Harry was constantly being defined in the media by who he may or may not have been cuddling up to. He was described as 'Lothario Harry' and the 'floppy haired hunk'. It didn't matter where in the world he was.

Rod Stewart of all people sort of confirmed that Harry had been briefly involved with his daughter, Kimberley, who had been at school in LA with Kim Kardashian. This was entirely different from his low-key dinner with Kendall – a well-orchestrated, dressed-up encounter that was all celebrity smiles for the cameras when they left Dan Tana's on Santa Monica Boulevard.

It didn't seem remotely a thing, although Rod did say that Harry's car was still parked outside his Beverly Hills mansion the next morning. The encounter seemed to attract more publicity for Rod, who had a new album coming out.

There was even less evidence of a secret fling with Nicole Scherzinger, the *X Factor* judge who had been present when One Direction had been assembled on the show. The fact that she was sixteen years older than Harry seemed to be the only reason for believing a 'source'. He was now being described as a 'pop hunk'.

He had much in common with Kendall thanks to their love of fashion and mutual friends in that world. They were part of the same small network including Cara Delevingne, who saw Kendall often on modelling jobs around the world.

They were even pictured wearing the same t-shirt with the logo CaKe on the front, a gentle rebuke to the media who love to merge two celebrity names together. Kim Kardashian and Kanye West (managed at the time by Irving Azoff) were Kimye; Harry and Taylor Swift were Haylor; and Harry and Kendall were Hendall.

Kendall, like Cara, had started modelling at a young age. In Harry, she also found somebody who understood what it was like to be thrust into the limelight as a teenager. Kendall was fourteen when she began modelling and soon featured as the cover girl of *American Cheerleader*. She credited cheerleading with helping her to overcome a natural shyness. It also helped that she was a fixture in *Keeping Up with the Kardashians*, the biggest reality TV show in the world.

The show began in 2007 when Kendall was eleven and only her half-sister Kim Kardashian could properly be considered well known; but it quickly made stars of the whole family: Kendall's parents, Kris and Caitlyn Jenner; her younger sister Kylie Jenner; her half-sisters, Kim, Kourtney and Khloe Kardashian; and her half-brother Rob Kardashian.

Kendall grew up on the show. She appeared only sporadically in the early years because she was attending the Sierra Canyon School, ten miles from where the family lived in Calabasas, an upmarket suburb of Los Angeles. There seemed no hurry to rush her dramatically into the public eye. That changed when she was the subject of a coming-of-age episode entitled 'Kendall's Sweet Sixteen' that centred around her birthday party and obtaining her driving licence. This was her launch pad to stardom.

Optimistically she had said that she and her younger sister wanted to keep 'somewhat normal lives' for a while. But when she met Harry, she already had her own clothing line, had been on the cover of *Miss Vogue* and *Harper's Bazaar* and was on the books of Wilhelmina Models.

Her career seemed to be moving faster than her love life. Right from the start she preferred to be guarded about any romances, perhaps a side-effect of having to live in front of a TV camera for part of her day. Harry was the first high-profile man she was linked to and that might have been a damp squib if they hadn't been seen together a few more times over the next couple of months.

'Together' usually meant editing out the friends and security that were with them. When they went on a skiing holiday to the Mammoth Mountain ski resort in Eastern California, it was an Azoff adventure. The problem Harry faced wherever he went in the world was that someone was bound to take his picture and either post it online or, less preferably, give it to a picture agency. He tried his best to stay in the shadows or make any picture half-baked. When he was in the mountains he was wearing head-to-toe ski wear and huge mirror sunglasses that practically covered his face. When pictures appeared online, nobody seemed interested that Jeffrey Azoff was in shot next to Harry.

He was snapped again with Kendall by a member of the audience at a concert by the Eagles, long-standing Azoff clients. You could just about make out Harry with his arm around Kendall, but it could have been anyone and the photographer failed to notice her mum Kris and sister Khloe who were sitting next to them.

Coincidentally, Khloe and Kris have been the only family members who have confirmed that Harry and Kendall did date for a while. Kris was appearing by Zoom on *The Ellen DeGeneres Show* in 2021 to talk about the end of *Keeping Up with the Kardashians*. She played a game of 'Never Have My Kids Ever'. The question was, 'Never have my kids ever dated someone from a boy band'. Kris held up a sign declaring 'They have.' Ellen then said, 'Well, of course, Kendall right. And Harry.' Kris said, 'Yeah.' It wasn't exactly chapter and verse.

Kendall wasn't with him when he popped over to the Sundance Film Festival in Utah but Jeffrey, who had now joined CAA (the Creative Artists Agency), was, as were Harry's friends from London, Alexa Chung and Pixie Geldof. This time Harry was properly dressed up for the camera, posing on the red carpet before the premier of *Wish I Was Here* with the film's star and director Zach Braff. The movie world was one completely removed from One Direction and one Harry was keen to join. Perhaps Jeffrey could help?

Finally, Harry turned twenty. He was in the US on the day and reportedly Kendall threw a party for him at Caitlyn Jenner's Malibu mansion. His new Los Angeles 'family' were there. It seemed as if he had been a teenager forever, accomplishing so much in the five years – and earning £10 million – since he had taken the day off from Holmes Chapel bakery to go to an audition. To mark the occasion, Directioners donated more than £5,000 to the Believe in Magic charity. Harry tweeted in response: 'Just saw donations to believeinmagicx for my birthday. Thank you. You're all very kind and nice. xx.'

Harry's gift to himself was rumoured to be a painting by the influential twentieth-century New York artist Jean-Michel Basquiat. All sorts of huge sums were floated about claiming to be the amount he paid for it at a Christie's sale but the art world decided it was £1.8 million. Harry was not tossing away his money on a whim. He was already renowned for being very smart with his fortune and art was recognised as a shrewd investment. Apparently the super-rich superstar Jay-Z had recommended it to Harry, but it could just as easily have been any of his new LA circle. They knew how to make a lot of money and how to hang on to it.

Basquiat has become one of the most sought-after artists, not least because he died tragically young at the age of twenty-seven in 1988. Cultural icons such as James Dean, Kurt Cobain and Jean-Michel Basquiat live forever if they leave us too soon. It's easy to see why the artist would appeal to Harry, because of his enduring reputation in the world of fashion. In 2005 he was listed in *GQ*'s '50 Most Stylish Men of the Past 50 years'; and in 2015 he was on the cover of *The New York Times Style Magazine*'s Men's Style Issue. In the 1996 biographical film of his life he was played by Emmy Award-winning actor Jeffrey Right while David Bowie took the role of Andy Warhol.

Harry has never confirmed that he owns a Basquiat but he was building up a private art collection. He had begun by reportedly buying a limited-edition portrait of Kate Moss by the peerless Banksy. He was conspicuous at the Art 13 fair at the Kensington Olympia. He was looking to decorate his London home with avant-garde pieces. He bought at least four random works, including a cast of a human skull placed upon a Bible, sat alongside a hypodermic needle; a work by renowned taxidermist Polly Morgan; some prints by south London artist Ben Turnbull; and, intriguingly, a sculpture for £20,000 depicting Jesus as a boxer, complete with boxing gloves and white shorts.

On another occasion Harry spent more than £33,000 on some twenty original pieces of artwork by Hayden Kays, the very collectable London artist said to straddle the gap between street art and high art. He is renowned for his typewriter works on love and sex and that's what Harry bought on a private visit to the Cobb Gallery round the corner from Nick

Grimshaw's place in London. As well as the world of fashion – and philosophy – Harry embraced the world of contemporary art in London.

Fashion was again the focus of his attention when he attended the 2014 London Fashion Show and watched Cara walk the runway at the Burberry Prorsum show. He deliberately gave Kendall's show a miss. She was the hit of the week when she walked in Giles Deacon's fall 2014 show. Her rising profile was clear when she was seated next to Anna Wintour, the Editor-in-Chief of *Vogue*, at the Topshop show.

Harry, it seemed, was mindful not to make he and Kendall the story at her big professional opportunities. They were about her. She did attend his belated British birthday at the uber-trendy Box Club in Soho, which Nick Grimshaw had helped to organise. For once the night out and the lurch home were not captured by the paparazzi. He wasn't pursued through the streets of London by men on motorbikes, so his legal fight seemed to be working.

He wasn't at the High Court in London the following month when his lawyer David Sherborne updated Mr Justice Dingemans on the legal action's progress. He was 'happy to inform' the judge that the four defendants involved had consented to permanent injunctions. The identity of other photographers that had harassed Harry was still being investigated. The solicitor added that it was hoped that because of the protection the courts had given the star, other individuals 'have in fact gone to ground and that is the last we hear of them'. Harry was keen for his legal team to emphasise again that he was not seeking a 'privacy injunction'; and he didn't want to stop fans approaching him in the street.

While this was a serious victory for Harry, he had been forced to confront the painful truth that certain aspects of celebrity life were not fun. The world contracted while friends you could trust became fewer. David Sherborne summed up what the legal success would achieve: '… an end to the crazy pursuit of the claimant when he is not on official duties.'

It would, however, soon be time to get back to those 'official duties'.

13

FOUR-D

Harry loves a flash car. When his pal Ed Sheeran passed his driving test and bought a Mini Cooper he told him not to be silly and to get an Aston Martin. He himself had splashed out $200,000 on a scarlet Ferrari California as soon as the money started pouring into his bank account. The convertible was the perfect ride for motoring around the streets of Beverly Hills.

He kept that car, along with his Range Rover Sport, for use in Los Angeles but in the UK he had invested, aged eighteen, in a dark grey Audi R8 Coupé that cost about £100,000 and was perfect for bombing up to Cheshire. It was the car he let his friends drive.

Harry also liked classic cars, buying a beautiful red Jaguar E-type Roadster that he would use to navigate his way around London. One of his first cars was the ultimate boy racer automobile, a white Ford Capri that was all the rage back in 1970. His vintage model of choice in LA was a white Mercedes.

He was behind the wheel of a Porsche when he drove up to the disused aircraft hangars in Cardington, Bedfordshire, where One Direction was rehearsing. He would be back on 'official duties' when the South American leg of the *Where We Are* tour began in the Colombian capital of Bogotá at the end of April 2014.

To prove his legal point about not seeking to stop fans approaching him, he was all smiles and posed for selfies when he was seen by some teenage girls. As soon as word got out the band was there it became the biggest local event for years, with hundreds gathering, hoping to catch a glimpse of one of the boys. The police were needed to keep a watchful eye on things. Harry cryptically tweeted that he was 'just hanging around today', which was the signal for the fans that he would be at the sheds.

This wasn't a repeat of the old-style bedlam when One Direction arrived at Heathrow. Mums turned it into a three-day social event, bringing their daughters, many of whom were under ten, to meet up with friends as if they were waiting for a glimpse of a member of the Royal Family.

The children would sing all the songs while they waited patiently. One mum, Dannii Ruff, who had brought her three children, observed, 'I am here because the kids wanted to come along – honestly! They spent two hours making all their posters. Everyone has been in a really good mood and when they've been driving off there's been no pushing or shoving from the crowd.' There was lots of screaming, though.

Harry always appreciated support from parents, who were, after all, bankrolling the tickets, the merchandise and everything connected with the group. At the press conference before the first show at the El Campin Stadium in the

Colombian capital, he said: 'I think with parents when they grow up they probably have a thing they were a fan of. I think they can relate to how their children feel. They get to relive it through their kids, which is quite nice.

'I think we put on a show where the parents come and enjoy it and they might not even be a fan of the music but they would say they've seen a good show.' They had their money's worth on the *Where We Are* tour. The band performed twenty-three songs, beginning with 'Midnight Memories' and ending with 'Best Song Ever'.

They had already played in front of more than 400,000 South American fans before the show moved to Europe, beginning with three nights at Croke Park in Dublin where Niall had first auditioned for *The X Factor*. The *Irish Independent* noted two strands to the band's audience – teenage girls and those still at primary school. The review was not exactly full of praise: 'While there's no shortage of energy – as you would expect from young men aged twenty and twenty-one – there just isn't the sort of U2-like showmanship that is necessary to make such a huge setting work.'

Was One Direction about to enter a phase of negative publicity? For once it wasn't Harry who hogged the headlines but Zayn and Louis. Footage emerged of them apparently smoking a rolled-up joint while in a car in Peru. A video was posted by the *Mail Online*, in which Louis is heard to say, 'So here we are, leaving Peru. Joint lit. Happy days,' before passing the suspicious cigarette to Zayn.

Liam, still the group's dad, issued an apology via Twitter: 'I love my boys and maybe things have gone a little sideways; I apologise for that. We are only in our twenties, we all do stupid things at this age. We all have a lot of growing up to do in extreme circumstance. I'm not making excuses but it's fact we are gunna fall short somewhere.'

Even Simon Cowell felt the need to give the band a positive comment: 'They're really respectful of their fans and they're a great British export … they've been a joy to work with … I've worked with lots of artists in the past who do lose the plot, who do lose respect for their fans, they've never done that.'

Harry said nothing about it but *The Sun* carried a story claiming that he was angry at the 'stupid and reckless' behaviour of his bandmates. Smoking a little weed was hardly grounds for being upset, although filming it might be thought to be stupid and reckless.

Perhaps more shocking to the Directioners was the strong rumour that Harry wanted to leave the band and strike out on his own. The dynamic within the group had subtly changed. Louis and Harry, for instance, didn't seem as close as they once were.

Louis would later explain that things became awkward between the two friends because of the constant rumours about the nature of their relationship. Conspiracy theorists online invented the name Larry Stylinson, an unwelcome variation on the Haylor label that had been given to Harry and Taylor Swift. Louis found it disrespectful to his girlfriend Eleanor Calder.

The fear that fans might question and analyse every minor interaction between him and Harry caused them to stay away from one another to a certain extent: 'It created this atmosphere between the two of us where everyone was looking into everything we did. It took away the vibe you get off anyone.'

Zayn confirmed that the constant scrutiny made it hard for Harry and Louis: 'They won't naturally go put their arm around each other because they're conscious of this thing that's going on, which is not even true. They won't do their natural behaviour.'

All the boys were far too professional for fans to notice any tension between them. They played three summer nights at Wembley Stadium. A crowd of 80,000 each night spent two hours queuing to get in. The London *Evening Standard* identified the band as Britain's most successful pop act of the twenty-first century. Tellingly, though, the headline in the newspaper referred to One Direction as 'Harry Styles and Co.'.

The band was filmed when they played the San Siro Stadium in Milan at the end of June. This time the director was Paul Dugdale, well regarded in the industry for his work with Adele, Coldplay and The Prodigy. Ben Winston and his partner at Fulwell 73, Leo Pearlman, were involved as executive producers. It wouldn't be the last time they would all work with Harry.

Subsequently, *Where We Are: The Concert Film* was shown in cinemas over a weekend in October when the American dates were completed. Over two days, it took an estimated $15 million worldwide, becoming the best-selling ever event cinema movie. The film was also the top trending topic on global Twitter, a further illustration that One Direction had no equals when it came to dominating the internet.

In her *Guardian* review, Leslie Felperin had an interesting view of Harry: complimenting him on his hair, she thought he had grown more handsome but 'he also looks like he can barely conceal his boredom. He's literally just going through the motions.' She added that it was surely only a matter of time before he went off to make that first solo album. Would she and many others who thought the same be proved correct?

The band was still on an annual conveyor belt: they needed to produce their fourth album during 2014 on the same shattering schedule as previous years. Julian Bunetta and John Ryan were heavily involved again but this time Liam and Louis were the most active songwriting members of the band and there was no blanket credit for all five on every track.

Harry's most memorable contribution was as co-writer of a track called 'Stockholm Syndrome'. He was the principal lyricist on a song that referenced the psychological attachment some captives experience towards their captors. Every song seems to have to be about a specific person or event and Harry said this was about a 'nympho' he had once known. Lyrically, it was an interesting song although the chorus 'Oh baby, look what you've done to me' was more boy band than Bowie.

The co-writers were Julian, John and the Swedish songwriter and producer Johan Carlsson, who had already worked with Harry. Together they had composed 'Just a Little Bit of Your Heart' for Ariana Grande. She recalled how it came about: 'I was at the studio one day and he was there, and literally, Johan and Savan [Kotecha] were like, "Hey, do you want to write something for Ariana?" And Harry was like "Sure, mate". And he just did.

'It's a beautiful song. He's an amazing writer. It's really beautiful. He's amazingly talented.'

The wistful ballad featured on her second album, *My Everything*, which was a US number one while One Direction's *Where We Are* tour was playing to packed stadiums around the States in the late summer of 2014. Intriguingly, Jeffrey Azoff and his partner, Glenne Christiaansen, went to several concerts on the tour. Glenne was also well known in the pop world as Snap Inc's Global Head of Music Partnerships.

Harry meanwhile had more than music on his mind, revealing the type of thoughtful individual he was becoming. When the band arrived in New Orleans in the last week of September 2014 to perform in front of 50,000 people at the Mercedes-Benz Superdome, he took the time to post on Twitter his support of the actor Emma Watson. Earlier in the week she had given the keynote address at the launch of UN Women's HeForShe initiative at the Museum of Modern Art (MoMA) in New York.

In front of an audience that included the then-UN Secretary General, Ban Ki-moon, the first female president of Finland, Tarja Halonen, and Meghan Markle before she met Prince Harry, Emma gave a rousing speech, pressing the point that gender equality was not just a 'woman's issue' but 'everyone's issue'.

Emma forcefully explained that in order for gender equality to be achieved, harmful and destructive stereotypes of masculinity and behavioural expectations for boys and men had to change. She urged, 'Both men and women should feel free to be sensitive. Both men and women should feel free to be strong.'

Her words inspired Harry, encapsulating the essence of non-toxic masculinity that he would come to embrace. He posted a picture of himself holding a handmade sign that

declared 'HEFORSHE'. Underneath he wrote, 'I'm supporting @UN Women and @EmWatson in HeForShe. As should
you.'

It was a simple, unexpected gesture. Harry's post was
retweeted 300,000 times and liked by nearly half a million
users. He had a powerful global presence.

HeForShe was new and exciting. A much older and more
familiar cause was Band Aid and One Direction took part in
the 2014 version to raise money to combat the Ebola crisis in
West Africa. The format hadn't changed since the original
recording thirty years earlier. Some of the biggest names in
music took part, including Chris Martin, Sam Smith and Ed
Sheeran. One Direction was handed the Paul Young role of
singing the first verse.

Harry was sporting his rock-star hair and a white shirt with
racing cars dotted all over it, but he seemed subdued and out
of sorts during the day at the Sarm Studios in Notting Hill. At
the 'post-match' interview the band were not their old
exuberant selves, giving rise to rumours that all was not well
within the group and they might be on the verge of splitting
or, at the very least, going on hiatus.

The new release was expertly sung by all, if perhaps, a little
more downbeat than the original. The song reached number
one in the UK, the only time One Direction topped the
singles chart that year. The album, *FOUR*, however, reached
the pinnacle on both sides of the Atlantic. This time round,
they became the first band to have their first four albums
debut at number one in the US.

As ever the reviews were mixed. *Time* magazine was very
positive, highlighting further evidence of the boys' 'maturation

into men'. It noted Harry's 'raspy swagger' and the 'spunky Styles-penned "Stockholm Syndrome"'. *Rolling Stone*, always big supporters of the group, was equally enthusiastic, declaring that One Direction had 'mastered the ancient boy-band art of whispering directly into listeners' ears'. Harry was described as a 'weapons grade hottie' but best of all, from his point of view, 'Stockholm Syndrome' was nominated as the album's brightest song: 'a slick, body-moving R&B ditty'.

Although *FOUR* didn't quite match the success of *Midnight Memories* it was still the sixth best-selling album of the year worldwide, with sales of 3.2 million. The tour, however, was a phenomenal success, with breathtaking figures. *Where We Are* was seen by nearly three and a half million people, generating gross receipts of more than $290 million.

But there would be very little time to bask in that success. Next year's stadium tour, called – accurately – *On the Road Again*, had already been announced with a fifth album needing to be written while on the road. Zayn, perhaps most of all, struggled with the rapid turnaround. He wanted a proper studio, not a makeshift one in a hotel room. He wanted to take his time.

The game was up as far as he was concerned when he completed some songs, including one called 'Pillowtalk', that were for him alone. It was thought that he wrote the song after the 'break' but that wasn't the case. A few years later Julian Bunetta would recall that Zayn played him the track in a smoky hotel room in Saitama, Japan. His verdict says it all: 'Fucking amazing!'

Three weeks later, Zayn was gone. The announcement came after the concert on 18 March 2015 at the AsiaWorld-

Arena in Hong Kong. His departure was brought on by stress and anxiety and he flew back to the UK to recover. In the official statement put out by the band on Facebook, he said, 'I want to be a normal 22-year-old who is able to relax and have some private time out of the spotlight. I know I have four friends for life in Louis, Liam, Harry and Niall. I know they will continue to be the best band in the world.'

That all sounded very reasonable but gradually that carefully constructed publicity line unravelled. In his very first interview after the split, he told *Fader* magazine that One Direction's music was as 'generic as fuck'. Two years later he admitted that he and Harry were not close while they were in the band. He revealed he 'never really spoke to Harry' and that he had never been under the impression they would keep in touch.

Harry has said very little about it, although he did say he thought it a shame that Zayn felt that way about One Direction's music. He wished him good luck in doing what he was doing. He did make one amusing reference to his now ex-bandmate when he guest-hosted *Saturday Night Live* in 2019. Recalling those boy-band days, he said, 'I love those guys, they're my brothers: Niall, Liam, Louis and, uh, Ringo, yeah, that's it.' People often forget that Ringo Starr was the first member of The Beatles to leave the group, if only for a short time.

Zayn's departure was actually perfect for Harry. While it had been widely assumed that he would be the first to leave, he would now not have that label on his back. He would not have to answer interminable questions about why he left. He would not face the natural disappointment of the millions of

The four faces of a budding superstar:

Top Left Cool: Harry does his best Bryan Adams impersonation as lead singer of his school band, White Eskimo.

Top Right Apprehensive: Harry wonders if Simon Cowell thinks he has the X Factor after he sings 'Isn't She Lovely' at his first televised audition in 2010.

Left Charismatic: The smile that melts a million hearts is already in place when Harry arrives at the BBC Radio 1 studios in Central London.

Below Excited: After singing Rihanna's 'Only Girl (In the World)', One Direction were within touching distance of the *X Factor* final.

The Harry hug: Throughout the UK promotional tour of 'What Makes You Beautiful', Harry showed he had a genuine connection with his fans.

In the modern world, every fan has a phone to capture a golden moment – Harry arrives at BBC Radio 1's Teen Awards at Wembley Arena in October 2012.

What Gareth Southgate missed – Harry shows off his skills at the Newcastle United training pitch in April 2013.

Harry looks as if he's strayed in from a different band when the remaining four members of One Direction attend the American Music Awards in Los Angeles in November 2015.

Harry has an inner circle of his closest friends: he greets James Corden at the Aquascutum show during London Fashion Week in February 2012.

Harry was often seen out and about in London with DJ Nick Grimshaw during the early years of One Direction.

Spot the celebrity: Harry fits right in among the front-row stars at the Burberry Prorsum show during London Fashion Week, September 2013, when supermodel Cara Delevingne has all his attention.

Growing up, Harry owed much of his enlightenment and empathy to the two most important women in his life. He clearly also inherited his winning smile from his mum, Anne, pictured with her son at the Sony Music BRITs afterparty in February 2013.

Harry has always praised his sister Gemma's intelligence, but she shares his eye for a fashionable outfit – looking elegant with him during the launch party of *Another Man* magazine at Albert's Club, London, in October 2016.

Harry jumped at the opportunity to introduce his hero, Stevie Nicks, when she was inducted into the Rock and Roll Hall of Fame for the second time in New York, March 2019. One day it might be the other way round.

In good spirits getting ready to play Spill Your Guts, Fill Your Guts with Kendall Jenner on *The Late Late Show* in December that year: his great pal Ben Winston, now the show's producer, is next to Kendall.

The Harry hug again. This time he joyfully embraces his manager Jeffrey Azoff after winning the Best Solo Performance Grammy for 'Watermelon Sugar' in March 2021.

The fashion icon: Harry models Gucci as co-host of the Met Gala in New York, May 2019.

He wore three outfits to the 2020 BRIT Awards, finishing the evening in a vibrant yellow Marc Jacobs suit.

This fabulous green feather boa makes the perfect accessory at the 2021 Grammys.

Perhaps the ultimate Gucci suit for the Red Carpet: at the BRIT Awards in May 2021 when he collected the Mastercard British Single award for 'Watermelon Sugar'.

Left: Director Christopher Nolan said Harry had 'an old-fashioned face', when he cast him as a beleaguered young soldier in the acclaimed war drama *Dunkirk*.

Below: Another period piece, this time set in the 1950s – playing Florence Pugh's husband in the psychological thriller *Don't Worry Darling*, in which he had the added bonus of indulging his passion for vintage luxury cars.

His hair was still the right length for *My Policeman*, starring alongside Emma Corrin.

Nothing about Harry Styles is uniform, except when filming his latest movie, *My Policeman*, in Brighton.

Harry cools off in beautiful Tuscany after finishing filming *My Policeman* in June 2021. At least he no longer had to spend an hour in make-up every morning covering his tattoos!

There's nothing better than a stroll after Sunday lunch, especially in the LA sunshine. Harry puts his arm around a happy Olivia Wilde after a meal with friends in their home neighbourhood of Los Feliz, in August 2021.

Directioners. Instead, he could knuckle down and put the fans first; there was a tour to finish and an album to make. And while all that was going on, he could quietly continue to plan for life after 1D.

PART THREE

A MODERN MAN

14

HISTORY

Los Angeles was becoming a home from home for Harry. His twenty-first birthday party in Hollywood was like an after-show night at the Oscars – there were so many stars who he could call friends. Kendall was there; and Cara; and Alexa; and Becks; and James; and the Azoffs.

Harry looked like a rock star, more heavy metal than boy band. He wore a black military-style jacket with a matching unbuttoned shirt. His hair was long, curly and casually messy. He couldn't stop smiling at Lola's Bar as he greeted guests who also included Chris Martin and Jennifer Lawrence, Kelly Osbourne and Rita Ora. His mum was back in the UK but Harry made sure they shared FaceTime from the party so that she could see what was going on and that he was enjoying himself on his birthday.

Adele, who had settled happily in Los Angeles, dropped by and gave him a signed copy of her iconic album *21* with a note just for him that said, 'I did some pretty cool stuff when I was twenty-one. Good luck!' Harry, who thought Adele was amazing, was understandably thrilled.

None of One Direction attended, unless they managed to sneak in and out and avoid any cameras. Niall, at least, had the excuse of being in Melbourne watching the Australian Open tennis. The supermodel Gigi Hadid, a great friend of Kendall and Cara, was there demonstrating again the small celebrity circles in which Harry moved. A few months later she would embark on a serious relationship with Zayn.

Harry was involved briefly with the Austrian model Nadine Leopold and she was at Lola's, although she didn't pose with him. Geographically the relationship was a non-starter, with Nadine based in New York, but they were seen by paparazzi shopping together in Beverly Hills and getting into his black Range Rover.

He wasn't back in Los Angeles again until May, after the Asian leg of the *On the Road Again* tour, when all anyone wanted to talk about was the Zayn drama. The now-four members of One Direction were booked to appear on *The Late Late Show with James Corden*, who had just taken over presenting the long-running late-night talk show from Craig Ferguson.

Harry's small world in London had now become his small world in Los Angeles. James had moved to California with his wife Julia and their young children. Ben Winston had moved too, becoming the executive producer on his show. The two old friends would become astonishingly successful in Hollywood in a very short space of time.

Harry was understandably delighted to have them close by in LA. There would always be somewhere to stay! When One Direction first appeared on *The Late Late Show*, it was too soon for Harry to make everything about him. Instead, he made sure he was very much part of the group, although he wasn't seated next to Louis. Instead, he was between Liam and Niall.

The rapport between Harry and James, who calls him Harold, was clear, especially when the host was trying to suggest he would have been the perfect replacement for Zayn. Harry was having none of it. Diplomatically, Liam said there were no hard feelings against their old bandmate. They had been a bit angry before experiencing a feeling of disappointment.

They had a laugh with James about the things that were thrown at them on stage, including the obligatory bra and pants, a hamburger and a dildo that almost hit Harry in the face. Louis admitted he preferred to sleep in the familiar surroundings of the tour bus rather than in an anonymous hotel room.

Perhaps of most interest was the news that Harry had been on a juice cleanse since they had arrived in LA. He admitted that he had been feeling 'gross' after flying so much while on tour. Although wellness was obviously not exclusively a California pursuit, Harry was embracing some of the aspects into his lifestyle.

He had taken up yoga and Pilates to help with a bad back. He had struggled with it for many years and hurling himself around a stage night after night didn't help. Sometimes he said the cause was his paper round back in Holmes Chapel when the bag was so heavy he would be lopsided on his bike. Other times he thought it was due to having one leg shorter than the other.

Yoga helped, particularly when they were on tour. He even tried Bikram Yoga, during which the room temperature is turned up very high to encourage the class to sweat. While in the Far East, he had started to meditate twice a day to properly rest his body and mind to cope with a schedule that was as demanding as ever.

Harry liked to party but readily understood that it was a one-way ticket to disaster if that's all you did on tour. He didn't sample the fleshpots of Bangkok, for instance, preferring to wander around some local markets and visit a Buddhist temple. There was more to his life than tequila.

The purpose of the break in LA was to promote the DVD of their concert film and to spend some studio time fulfilling their contract for a fifth album. For a change they had a few weeks to just write songs. 'It was just the coolest time to sit and think,' reflected Harry. 'It gave us the chance to focus on writing good songs that we like and we wanted to listen to.'

Harry's most memorable contribution was a wistful ballad called 'If I Could Fly', which became a big favourite among Directioners and one he would play live in the future when he began touring as a solo artist. As always, the fans wanted to know who Harry was missing in the melancholic lyric. He didn't say.

Instead, he explained that love songs did not have to be about one specific person. They should not always be taken too literally: 'They can be about a time or a place and you kind of personify it and stick a name on it and then everyone thinks it's about a certain person but I don't think it's always so black and white.'

Sometimes Harry was merely the observer. He explained, 'You can write a great love song about two people you're not.' He wrote or co-wrote two other songs, 'Perfect' and 'Olivia'. Again, he declined to say who, if anyone, the songs were about.

The principal difference between *Made in the AM*, as it would be titled, and the previous album was that the band knew it would be the last – at least for a very long time. Julian Bunetta, who again was very involved in writing and producing the album with John Ryan and fellow LA-based songwriter and producer Jamie Scott, confirmed that the vibe was different this time round. But he did notice how much they had all grown as songwriters and musicians.

One Direction soon had to leave Los Angeles for Cardiff when the *On the Road Again* tour resumed at the Millennium Stadium, as the Principality Stadium was then called. This was the first time the UK had seen them perform as a four-piece. While Zayn's easy high notes might have been missed by connoisseurs, the fans were as excited as ever, responding enthusiastically when the band instituted a screaming contest. The boys chatted to each other about the time they had first played the Welsh capital as part of the *X Factor* tour four years earlier – time really had flown by.

The *Daily Telegraph* thought their charm and personality was arguably their greatest asset, maintaining a 'kind of shambling boy-next-door amateurism at the heart of a slick, stadium-scale production'. But a more passionate review came from a devoted fan in her online blog. She burst into tears before they came on stage and spent the whole concert 'bawling her eyes out'. She concluded: 'I'm still wishing I could go back to that day and relive it.' As Harry said, 'We're not us if you're not you.'

They were back in the US at the end of August, performing at Soldier Field in Chicago when news leaked that they would be taking a break when the current tour finished.

Harry unofficially became a muse when he stepped out for a party during the second London Fashion Week in late September 2015. He looked very different as he arrived for *Love* magazine's Miu Miu brand event at Loulou's private members club in Mayfair. He was seen out for the first time in an eye-catching Gucci suit.

Quietly, he had been adopted by Italian-born Alessandro Michele, the game-changing creative director of the legendary label. A graduate of Rome's Academy of Fashion and Costume, he grew up with a love and appreciation for museums, art, antiquity and the romance of classic cinema.

Alessandro, who looks like a cross between Jesus and a member of the Grateful Dead, had set the fashion world buzzing at the first London Fashion Week that year in February when, at five days' notice, he produced the Gucci runway show. Originally, he had been hired to design handbags, before progressing to be the accessories designer, and then was called up to take charge of the prestigious London show.

Vogue Runway noted the collection's androgynous languor and, more relevantly as far as Harry would be concerned, its 'blurred gender divide'. At the time Gucci badly needed a boost amid reports of plunging sales. Alessandro was tasked with turning its fortunes around and nothing would benefit that ambition more than an association with one of the most popular pop stars in the world. Alison Jane Reid observed, 'Harry's partnership with Gucci is a marriage of celebrity and heritage. He is one of the biggest artists on the planet and when he wears Gucci that generates a huge amount of press, interest and cachet in the brand which directly leads to sales.'

His first public Gucci was a bold geometric-designed suit worn over an Yves Saint-Laurent black shirt. Alison Jane thought it a visual masterpiece: 'It's the look of the dandy rock star who likes to take a trip back to the sixties and seventies.' If it was a trial run then the public reaction was very encouraging. The floral suit he wore to the 2015 American Music Awards – the AMAs – was even bolder. While his bandmates looked sombre in dark well-tailored suits, Harry literally stole the red carpet. His suit, again worn over a black shirt and, this time, a black bolo (shoestring) tie was all anyone was talking about the next day, which was job done.

Alison Jane Reid was impressed: 'He looks extraordinary. Flamboyance and flower power suits him. It's about showmanship, whimsy and fantasy. The rest of the band appear so dull in comparison.' Not everyone took his new look seriously, some suggesting that it resembled some curtains or a bedspread you could pick up from Ikea.

Few people realised at the time that Harry now had a personal stylist. Harry had his own ideas and Alessandro produced the eye-catching wardrobe, but it was a young British stylist, Harry Lambert, who was responsible for the whole 'look' – from the way he wore his hair to the shiny black boots on his feet. Without any fanfare, the other Harry is arguably the most important figure in his client's journey to genuine fashion icon.

Lambert was the man who thought it was time for something new. He wanted the boy band pop star to be bold and be noticed more. Harry Styles was the first famous celebrity to wear one of Alessandro's catwalk creations on the red carpet. Lambert believed this was a turning point for Harry. He observed, 'It was very exciting to see everyone's responses, but also how great he looked in it.'

Lambert is very much a behind-the-scenes figure. He had been working with Harry since 2013 when they met during London Fashion Week. Just as the young Harry Styles had done in Holmes Chapel, Lambert grew up in his home town of Norwich with a love of clothes. He was the teenager dressing the mannequins in his local charity shop and who marvelled at the provocative costumes of Madonna.

His first thought was to be behind the camera, and he achieved First Class Honours in photography at the University College for the Creative Arts (UCCA) in Rochester, Kent. He realised, though, that it was styling the subjects for photographs that he preferred, so he did an internship with British *Vogue* before working directly as an assistant to one of the magazine's stylists.

There, Harry worked closely with a flotilla of young, go-ahead photographers, gaining a reputation that led to him being one of the judges at the Elite Model UK competition. He also worked for leading brands including Topman and Tommy Hilfiger. He was recognised within the industry but didn't have any celebrity clients until he met Harry Styles, a blank canvas who seemed willing to try anything. They shared the same relaxed outlook about fashion, which is why they both found the criticism of his AMA suit so funny.

His outfit almost overshadowed the band's second consecutive victory in the premier award category, Artist of the

Year. They were also named favourite group in the pop/rock category. It was old friends' night, with Ed Sheeran picking up favourite male artist and Ariana Grande winning favourite female artist. Taylor Swift won album of the year for *1989* – widely believed to have been mostly about Harry – but she wasn't at the Microsoft Theater on the night.

One Direction performed 'Perfect' on stage, which was very much an archetypal One Direction song – beautifully sung verses followed by an anthemic chorus that everyone in the audience could sing along to, whether in tune or not. At the time it was their latest release, the second single from *Made in the AM* after 'Drag Me Down'. The video for 'Perfect', directed by the renowned Sophie Muller, was a diverting snapshot of their life on the road. Beautifully shot in black and white at the InterContinental Hotel in New York, it showed them passing the time – Niall practised his golf-putting; they kicked a ball around; they looked at the skyline; ran down the corridors with their security or just sat about. Mostly, Harry wore a killer patterned shirt, but there's one quick scene where his stylist, Harry Lambert, is helping him put on a jacket.

'Perfect' was part of the publicity drive to coincide with the release of *Made in the AM*. For the first time a One Direction album did not debut at number one in the US, beaten to the top spot by Justin Bieber's *Purpose*. That scenario was reversed in the UK. Worldwide, *Made in the AM* sold more than 2.4 million copies and was the sixth best-selling album of the year.

Harry was determinedly upbeat, describing it as 'the best album we feel we've done'. Zayn said he didn't buy it. *NME* were unimpressed, describing the album as 'pretty silly' and suggesting that the band had 'shown their age'. (Harry was twenty-one.) The review concluded, tongue-in-cheek, 'Now they can get on with the fall-outs, drug binges, bankruptcy and podginess.'

More positively, *Rolling Stone*, always great supporters of the band, commended the album as 'the kind of record the world's biggest pop group makes when it's time to say thanks for the memories'. *USA Today* singled out 'Perfect' as an 'exemplary pop song' and praised the band's defiance and maturity; but the writer, Patrick Ryan, also made the point: 'It's tough to promote a new album when everyone's marked your gravestone.'

They had to soldier on for a little longer. They were back with James Corden for Tattoo Roulette, in which either Niall, who didn't have one, or Harry, who was covered in them, were going to lose. Harry lost and during a commercial break had 'Late Late' tattooed on his left arm. James referred to Harry as a good sport and he was a natural for what makes good TV. During the 'Never Have I Ever' game on *Ellen*, the question was 'Never have I ever made out with someone double my age'. He responded with good humour, 'What is this game?!'

The very last concert, if you can call it that, was when they were the guests on James Corden's popular Carpool Karaoke in December. Harry was wedged in the back seat of a Range Rover between Liam and Louis. There was no knock-about banter between them. With James, who has a good voice, they sang 'What Makes You Beautiful', 'Story of My Life', 'No Control', 'Perfect' and 'Drag Me Down'. The video has been watched nearly 184 million times on YouTube.

Just before that was broadcast in the US, they had jetted over to London to appear, fittingly, as the special guests on the live final of Season 12 of *The X Factor*. It was old pals' day for Harry. Simon Cowell and Cheryl were there as usual but they were joined by new judges Rita Ora and Nick Grimshaw. Olly Murs, who had been a support act for them on tour, presented alongside Caroline Flack.

Harry stood centre stage, in a red floral Gucci suit that had already become a trademark look for him. Five years after their own final on the show, they sang 'History' from the new album: 'We got a whole lot of history' … and they had.

15

AN OLD-FASHIONED FACE

———

The first thing that had to go was the hair. Harry needed a military clip for his role as Alex in the epic World War II drama *Dunkirk*. He couldn't look like a rock star if he was meant to be a soldier crawling along a beach in Northern France. At least any decision about a new look as a solo artist was taken out of his hands. He was philosophical about the short back and sides: 'We had to make the chop,' he said. 'I felt very naked but it was good! It's very breezy.'

He first auditioned for the film in February 2016. It wasn't just a whim, waking up one morning and deciding to try out for one of the biggest movies of the year. Behind the scenes Business Team Harry had been assembled to take over formally as soon as the final commitments to One Direction had been fulfilled. The announcement that he was leaving Modest Management and joining Jeffrey Azoff at CAA was made just six weeks after Simon Cowell had wished the band a fond farewell on *The X Factor*.

Modest, run by music stalwarts Richard Griffiths and Harry Magee, were gracious about the train of events and said, 'We wish Harry the very best. It has been a real pleasure working with him. Harry is a total gentleman and we know our good friend Jeffrey Azoff will look after him. We look forward to sharing some great wine with them next time we are in LA.'

The next step was Jeffrey Azoff's departure from CAA a couple of weeks later to set up his own company, Full Stop Management. Harry was his star first client. The Creative Artists Agency remained his agents and it was through them that he was sent along to his first audition for the new Christopher Nolan blockbuster. He has kept very quiet about any coaching in Hollywood he may have received. His agents sent a tape of Harry acting to the casting director and he was invited along to a workshop audition.

All any of the hopefuls knew was that the movie would be about the evacuation from Dunkirk in 1940, one of the most famous events of World War II. Nobody was concerned about the lack of information, because London-born Nolan was one of the biggest name directors in Hollywood, famed the world over for his three Batman films, *The Dark Knight Trilogy*.

Harry was already a fan of Chris, as he called the director, because he had loved *Memento*, his acclaimed breakthrough thriller starring Guy Pearce as an amnesiac victim. Harry observed, 'I think I always found his structure so interesting and in terms of the way he keeps stuff from the audience when the characters don't know about it and it hits you so much harder.'

He also appreciated the director's ability to involve the audience in what is happening: 'You always feel you're right alongside the character, rather than watching a film of stuff happening to them.' That would be of particular significance in his new movie that transported us to the beaches alongside the desperate soldiers.

Harry didn't even know what part he was up for when he arrived for his first audition since his *X Factor* journey began back in 2010. He was in a group of other young actors who were making their way in their profession by more traditional methods.

One of them, Olivier Award winner Jack Lowden, remembers the day when Harry joined them at the workshop: 'Of course I knew who he was. When he walked into the audition, I was like "Whoa, that's Harry".'

The process that day was best described as a round robin, with the actors reading for different parts so that Nolan could see who was best suited to certain roles. Harry recalled chatting to another hopeful, Fionn Whitehead, who would end up being cast as the everyman soldier, Tommy, whose story starts and ends the film.

Fionn and Harry would become great friends. The film was a breakthrough for Fionn, who had been working in a coffee shop while Harry was touring the world. At nineteen, he was even younger than Harry, but like the pop star, his hair was much too long and curly for the part and needed to be sorted out.

While the young actors all knew of Harry Styles, the director himself said he hadn't realised just how famous his new cast member was. Christopher admitted, 'I mean, my daughter had talked about him but I wasn't really that aware of it. I cast Harry because he fit the part wonderfully and truly earned a seat at the table.'

One of the qualities that Harry possessed that raised him above most of the other actors at the workshop was his old-fashioned face. 'He has the kind of face that makes you believe he could have been alive in that period,' observed Christopher.

The excitement of the younger generation at the prospect of Harry Styles the film star was echoed by the eleven-year-old niece of the theatrical heavyweight Mark Rylance, who had a major role in the film. He remarked, 'She was just more excited than anything I've ever done because I was going to be acting with Harry Styles. I went up in her estimation.'

Mark was just one of many well-known actors in a cast that included Kenneth Branagh, Tom Hardy and Cillian Murphy. The prospect of working alongside such luminaries was daunting even for a man who had performed in front of millions.

Harry started training for his part of young soldier Alex. The movie would primarily be made in Northern France between July and September 2016, so he had some time to prepare. He had always enjoyed swimming in the Hampstead ponds near his North London home, but this was entirely different.

Harry was sent to Dunkirk two weeks early to train as a soldier alongside Fionn and the Welsh actor Aneurin Barnard. Surprisingly, he wasn't actually asked if he could swim until the day before they set off. This was a proper bootcamp, not one where they hung out rehearsing songs. Now he had to swim in the sea wearing an overcoat and carrying a pack.

Understandably, Harry was nervous, at least when filming began. He was in awe of a director of Christopher's reputation: 'You definitely feel like you don't want to let him down.

It's a big part of the nerves.' Harry was frank about how he felt in an interview with *The Big Issue*. He recalled that he was surprised by the sheer scale of the production: 'You walk on set the first day and get taken aback by everything.'

Christopher deliberately chose young, inexperienced actors such as Harry and Fionn so that everything they said and did would appear fresh and a new experience for them. At the end of one scene on his first day, the director turned to Harry and said, 'Congrats on your first close-up.' He gave him confidence in what he was doing. 'He never makes you feel like you have to try too hard.'

Harry plays one of the young soldiers desperately trying to reach England from Dunkirk by boat. It was an unglamorous role in an unglamorous film that reflected the sombre enormity of what actually took place in 1940, when more than 338,000 allied troops were rescued by an assembled potpourri of 800 boats.

Harry's opening line in a film was delivered with a mouthful of toast and jam :'What's wrong with your friend?' He has quite a few lines but they are mostly short sentences, although he delivers 'For fuck's sake!' with vigour and manages to get his tongue around, 'If he does, it's in an accent thicker than sauerkraut sauce.'

Sometimes Harry happily admits he didn't really know what was going on. One day his character was in the water near a boat when all hell was let loose: 'There was a boat blowing up as you were swimming, there were bullet noises everywhere, there was fire, people screaming … There was a lot going on. There was a bit where you're like, are we filming? What just happened?'

That wasn't the scariest part of filming. He discovered being under water, especially for a long scene, created a natural sense of panic. He explained, 'While you're down there filming and acting out the scene, you're also thinking, "I cannot breathe for much longer".'

Harry put any hardship he and his fellow actors may have faced into perspective, comparing it to the soldiers' ordeal. He observed, 'When you watch the film, it puts it in context what these guys might have actually gone through. It was so real. And it makes it very difficult to complain about what we might have gone through for a few hours.'

Harry endeared himself to the cast and crew by not playing the 'big I am' on set. He may have had security discreetly on hand to make sure no fans turned up to disrupt filming but that was as far as he took his star status. His modesty is almost as much of a trademark as his fashion choices. Christopher noted that Harry just enjoyed being part of the ensemble: 'Like the soldiers they played, the actors were all in it together and supported each other very well.'

This is not a film in which the heroes bask in triumph and are welcomed home with a tickertape parade. There were no winners at Dunkirk – only survivors. It's a film that almost exclusively features male characters. Only two women have brief speaking parts – one a nurse and the other waving at Kenneth Branagh from a rescue boat. Having Harry Styles in the film ensured that thousands of young women who might have given a grim war movie a miss would be queuing up to see it at their local cinema.

Unsurprisingly, most of the publicity surrounding the film centred on Harry, but the hype was controlled and he made sure he didn't overplay his role, keeping his interview responses quite bland: 'I feel incredibly lucky to have been a part of such an amazing story. I really enjoyed it. It was a good experience.'

The reviews for the film were exceptional and Harry was mentioned favourably in most of them. The *Independent* said, 'Styles is very competent and his performance does not stick out like a sore thumb as many feared.' *Rolling Stone* observed that he played a small role with 'subtle grace and zero pop star showboating'. *Glamour* magazine thought he was 'too darn handsome to play an undernourished, exhausted soldier'. NPR (National Public Radio) meant it as praise when pointing out that he didn't stand out in the part 'except for being a little handsomer than anyone else'.

One thoughtful point made by *Insider* online was that you could appreciate the movie without thinking, 'Hey, that's Harry Styles.' To achieve that, it was very important that Harry didn't sing. Ed Sheeran, for instance, did not receive universal applause after he sang during an episode of *Game of Thrones*. He looked and sounded exactly like Ed Sheeran. Fortunately, Harry did not lead his stricken comrades in a beach chorus of 'Kumbaya'.

His co-stars answered questions about Harry with good grace, recognising that he didn't ask for any of it. Jack Lowden observed, 'I feel like if he wants to act, then why shouldn't he! It's a very brave thing to just jump straight in like he has.' Fionn summed it up, 'The media have put too much emphasis on this one guy instead of the piece as a whole and the ensemble as a whole.'

Just how much Harry Styles added to the film's box office is impossible to guess. The film was the most successful World

War II movie of all time, grossing worldwide $522 million on an estimate budget of $100 million. More importantly perhaps, it was widely regarded as a masterly film, although it lost out on the Best Picture award at the Oscars to *The Shape of Water*.

Christopher Nolan said he thought Harry was a natural actor and would work with him again in the future. Harry commented drily that he definitely improved his swimming while shooting the film but would not commit to any future acting, declaring that he was 'one and done'. That, of course, stopped any speculation.

The beauty of making a film was that it could fuel interest in Harry's solo musical career, too. The public and media interest could all tie in together, presenting him in a completely different light from his image as one member of a boy band – make the film, record the album, release the album, release the film. Harry's next job was to actually write the album.

16

THE PINK ALBUM

———

After spending what seemed like years up to his neck in the English Channel, Harry chose the ideal spot to recharge the batteries and get away from it all – the sun-kissed Caribbean island of Jamaica. It wasn't all play, however; there was the serious business of writing songs and, just as importantly, finding the right tone and direction for the first solo album.

Harry took with him the recently assembled Team Styles – the group of super-talented musicians, writers and producers who had been working with him on his solo music project in Los Angeles before he set out on his filming adventure. He had made a clean break from everyone connected with One Direction.

The only throwback to the old days when he checked in to the Geejam writing and recording retreat in Port Antonio on the north-eastern coast of the island was a song called 'Two Ghosts'. He had written the track with Julian Bunetta and John Ryan in 2013 but had kept it in his back pocket, believing it would need some extra attention in the future.

'Two Ghosts' is a break-up song and at the time One Direction had another Harry slice of melancholia, the plaintive 'If I Could Fly', so it made extra sense to hang on to this one, especially as amateur sleuths reasoned it was about Taylor Swift and that debate would have been a distraction when *Made in the AM* was released.

The song begins 'same lips red, same eyes blue', which many assumed was a reference to her. Harry never said, and when pressed about it by Nick Grimshaw on Radio 1, let out a little scream and called for Jeffrey Azoff to help him out. 'I think it's pretty self-explanatory' was all he would say.

Such speculation always attracts interest in a song. It's a tried-and-tested publicity device that Taylor herself has used many times. Much of the album *1989* was said to be about Harry, including one track entitled 'Style'.

'Two Ghosts', as Harry explained, explores a universal theme about two people changing and growing apart. Musically the track represented a more mature sound for Harry, in line with his desire to hark back to the classic eras of the past where Joni Mitchell, Fleetwood Mac and Pink Floyd would jostle for favouritism in vinyl record collections.

But it was only one song and enjoying the peace and tranquillity of the Caribbean was not getting the other nine he needed for the album written. Harry's Jamaican entourage was led by the Grammy Award-winning producer Jeff Bhasker, a well-respected figure in LA music circles.

Jeff was a very accomplished musician, having studied at the Berklee College of Music in Boston. His entrance into the music business came as the keyboardist with Kanye West and, subsequently, as his musical director. He was far from being just a hip-hop specialist, however, and won Grammys for his work with Fun on the number one 'We Are Young' and on the equally successful 'Uptown Funk' by Mark Ronson.

He was a big name for Harry to have in his corner, but Jeff was initially unsure if the association was right for him. He asked Harry round for an initial chat and to give him the sniff test. His dog was notorious for biting people but Harry seemed completely unfazed when given the wary eye by the pet. He pointed his finger at him and the dog walked over and started licking it. Jeff recalled, 'That was when I was like, "This guy has something special".'

Harry already had a good idea of the direction he wanted his solo music to take. He brought round some examples, or 'references' as he called them, so that Jeff could hear the type of music that inspired him – there were no big Swedish anthems. Instead, he played him The White Stripes, the peerless American rock duo. At first Jeff thought Harry was playing his own actual demos and was mightily impressed until he realised it was the genuine article. He was still excited with the direction Harry wanted to take with his music.

Jeff was in his early forties with a young family, so he was keen to share the load. He brought in Alex Salibian and Tyler Johnson, both of whom had originally been his assistant before moving on to producing roles within his company, Kravenworks. The idea was to form a band around Harry that would become a creative unit.

Jeff wasn't there at the first day, which had been back in Venice, Los Angeles, before Harry's *Dunkirk* commitment. A new studio engineer, Ryan Nasci, joined Alex and Tyler to welcome Harry. They had arranged for a guitar player to join them but he failed to show. Ryan piped up that his roommate was a guitarist and he could give him a call. The man in question, Mitch Rowland, was working as a dishwasher in a pizza restaurant but could come in the next day. Mitch was in a local band and Tyler had already seen him play a kind of seventies rock guitar that would fit perfectly with what Harry wanted.

Mitch, who had recently moved to LA from his native Ohio, had never been in a recording studio before. He'd never heard of Harry Styles. Jeff recalled, 'Mitch comes down and the second he plugged in his guitar and started playing, Harry's eyes just lit up and he was like, "This is the guy".' Mitch would become Harry's new best friend in California.

Harry's admiration for Mitch increased when he discovered he was an accomplished drummer as well. Everyone, it seemed, could play, so Harry had an instant band with whom he could write and record his first album. After a couple of days, Mitch said he couldn't come in tomorrow because he had a shift at the pizza parlour. 'Well, you might not need to do that anymore,' said Harry.

Alex, a classically trained musician, acted as musical director, but Harry had taken the lead on the first morning and was the boss. During his time with One Direction he had improved his musical skills, playing guitar with Niall and practising on any piano he came across. As a result he could make far more of a contribution to songwriting than just a smart line to start things off. He was creative and involved every step of the way.

While there was a flurry of songwriting at the outset of the Instant Harry Band, he felt they needed to have some weeks with no other distractions, which is why he suggested Jamaica. Artists including Drake, Florence and the Machine, Katy Perry and Lily Allen have all found Geejam an idyllic place to work and play. Even the legendary artist Banksy was a guest one year.

Harry and the gang were there to work 90 per cent of the time and play was limited to watching rom-coms on Netflix in the evening. Then it was back to the studio, even if it was two o'clock in the morning. Jeff Bhasker, who had pretty much seen it all, was energised by the informality and immediacy of the way they were working.

Jeff was particularly impressed with Harry's clever wit and how well-read he was. Harry has been modest about his intelligence, preferring to applaud his sister for her academic achievements, but brains and the ability to absorb cultural influences was something he brought to the table – whether discussing philosophy with Alain de Botton or poetry with his producer.

Harry was appreciative of the work of the renowned Los Angeles poet and novelist Charles Bukowski, who was born in Germany but grew up in the US. He chronicled the tribulations of the less-advantaged in LA, where he spent most of his life. In the land of Hollywood, he described the ordinary lives of poor Americans.

A fan once threw a copy of *You Get So Alone at Times That It Just Makes Sense* for Harry on stage at the Gillette Stadium near Boston during One Direction's *Where We Are* tour. Harry picked up the book, stopped the concert – in front of 80,000 people – for a moment or two and quietly read a passage from the book of poetry that Bukowski wrote in later life. It contained observations that could resonate across the generations. 'Regret is mostly caused by not having done anything.'

Harry and Jeff would talk of Bukowski's gritty realism and his ability to speak from the heart. That was the direction they both wanted for the album. During one session after lunch, Harry started playing them a melody on the piano. He already had a lyric. Mitch and Ryan jumped all over it to flesh out the sound and, with Jeff now on the piano, Harry started singing. Mitch played guitar and drums, Ryan took the bass and three hours later they had made the first cut of 'Sign of the Times'.

The lyric was not a slice of whimsy but a thoughtful commentary on the things that matter in the world, especially equal rights for all, written by a man with a developing social conscience. The basis for the song was the story of a mother giving birth to a child and being told that she only has five minutes to live: she has to tell her child to stop crying and have the time of their life. The final song was an epic six minutes of sensitivity including the memorable line: 'You can't bribe the door on your way to the sky.'

His original version of the song contained the words 'Why are we always fucking running from the bullets?' One of the team suggested ditching the f-word in favour of 'stuck with' which sounded just as good and reduced the risk of anyone being offended by the song.

Jamaica wasn't all work. The team's two-storey hilltop villa was luxurious and Harry could begin his working day by going for a swim in a quiet, out-of-the-way cove where he was unbothered by anyone or anything – exactly what he wanted from this island interlude.

A film, *Behind the Music*, showing the making of the album revealed Harry to be quite drunk on one occasion after he enjoyed a few cocktails at the local Bush Bar after recording. He jumped over a bridge and landed in the water fully clothed.

Most of the album was written in Jamaica, but back in Los Angeles, Harry was still one song short. For a complete change, he went on a blind date with a student from Greenwood, South Carolina, called Townes Adair Jones. She had moved to California to study French and philosophy at UCLA. Apparently her sister, the actress Gilland Jones, made the arrangement.

Harry enjoyed the evening and next morning, seeking inspiration for one last song, decided to write about the experience. The clues that this was a girl from out of town were clear from the lyrics. She was also a big reader who had a book for every situation – though he didn't say if they talked about Bukowski or Alain de Botton.

As usual, Harry refused to be drawn on her identity but he did admit that her name, 'Townes', was in the song, which rather gave the game away. Harry had created a little piece of mystery which acted as publicity catnip for the media when he was promoting the record. Townes herself, who is named after her father, has never spoken about Harry, although a 'friend' was quoted as saying she loved the song but didn't want any attention.

Now the album was finished other than the all-important final mix, the title had to be finalised as well as the choice of first single. Provisionally the first Harry Styles album was going to be called *Pink*. He often quoted the observation from the artist Paul Simonon, bass player with The Clash, that, 'Pink is the only true rock and roll colour.' One major drawback was that one of the biggest artists in the world was called Pink so it might be confusing, and the superstar didn't need any free advertising. *Sign of the Times* was also a non-starter because it was already the title of a classic album by Prince.

So they went with *Harry Styles* as the title, which was obvious, accurate and left no doubt that this was the first solo album. He decided to take it with him on a trip back to the UK so he could play it to his family. His mum liked it and cried happily at her son's achievement. Unfortunately, there was some sad news. Louis Tomlinson's mother Jay had died from leukaemia at the age of fifty-two. Jay had become a great friend of Harry's mum in particular, but he too had always enjoyed her company. Privately, there were also concerns regarding the failing health of his much-loved stepfather Robin.

Having chosen the album title, the next job was selecting the first single, which would act as the most important tool in the promotion of the album. There was little argument where Harry was concerned – it was always going to be 'Sign of the Times'. The only dilemma was whether to edit a radio version of the six-minute song.

Fortunately, the boss of Columbia Records, Rob Stringer, decided they should definitely go with the long cut. He was a great supporter of Harry, in much the same way as he had nurtured Adele through the early days of her first album, *19*. Harry was rumoured to have signed with the One Direction label, a subsidiary of Sony, back in the summer of 2016, but it wasn't until the following February that Rob confirmed that his company would be releasing *Harry Styles*.

Following the end of their contracts as 1D, Harry was the only member of the band that signed with their existing label.

Harry, who was always aware of a business opportunity, started his own record label, Erskine Records, which would release his output under the Columbia umbrella. His personal assistant, Emma Spring, who kept well away from the limelight, was named as the company director. He called it Erskine after Erskine House, a large property next to Hampstead Heath and the sixteenth-century Spaniards Inn. Harry already had two companies in his name – HSA Publishing and Rollcall Touring.

While the whole world seemed to know 'Sign of the Times' was coming, the first time it was heard in full was on its day of release in the UK at the beginning of April 2017. Nick Grimshaw played it on his Radio 1 breakfast show when Harry was his special guest. The release coincided with Rob Stringer being appointed as chief executive of Sony Records, the parent company of Columbia, making him an even more powerful ally.

Harry performed the song for the first time for a television audience on *Saturday Night Live*, the long-running late-night US show. He had a very good relationship with *SNL*. One Direction had appeared on the show three times but this was his first time as a guest without the band. It was a tour de force and he showed he had comedic flair and didn't mind sending himself up. He started off by dancing and singing his way through 'Let's Dance' by David Bowie during host Jimmy Fallon's opening monologue.

The highlight was his hilarious impression of Mick Jagger as a contestant on *Celebrity Family Feud*, dressed in a white suit and employing all the over-the-top mannerisms of the Rolling Stone. 'Why would anyone in a successful band go solo? That is insane!' said Harry in his best Mick voice. Lastly, he was in a Civil War sketch as a Confederate soldier when a downbeat Civil War song turned into a boy-band number. He even dealt with his stick-on beard becoming unstuck in a slapstick way.

The serious point of the show was to showcase two new songs. He began with 'Sign of the Times', negotiating his way past some very high notes, dressed in a Gucci patterned suit. His band had now changed to the musicians who would play live with him. Mitch was still there, laidback as ever, but he couldn't play drums as well as lead guitar, so fortunately his girlfriend Sarah Jones was a superb drummer and was able to take over the sticks.

Mitch and Sarah had met in the pizza parlour where he worked and hit it off discussing music. Sarah, originally from Hereford, was an experienced touring drummer, playing with Bat for Lashes, Bloc Party and the synth pop band Hot Chip. She had also released her own records as Pillow Person. They would have to get used to Harry sleeping over at their house.

This particular episode of *Saturday Night Live* was the first to go live coast to coast, so it was the best possible showcase for the new material. Harry played guitar for the second song, 'Ever Since New York', which was an interesting choice as it's a downbeat, world-weary reflection on love and loss and a throwback to the seventies folk rock of the Eagles. He didn't choose to play his favourite track from the album, 'From the Dining Table', which he liked because, he said, it was the most personal.

Harry sang 'Sign of the Times' for the first time in the UK on *The Graham Norton Show*. It was a powerful and confident performance – a step up from the initial outing on *SNL*, with more smiles and less grimaces. The audience shrieked.

On the couch afterwards he sat next to Rob Brydon and was a good sport when Graham played a game of Warren Beatty Deadpan – a sort of true or false depending on the guest's ability to keep a straight face. Taking a slice of carrot cake along to present to Stevie Nicks on her birthday in 2015 when he took Gemma to a Fleetwood Mac concert at the O2 turned out to be true; catching chlamydia from a koala was definitely not true; and auditioning for the role of the next Hans Solo was a maybe.

'Sign of the Times' went to number one in the UK charts on its release, knocking Ed Sheeran's 'Shape of You' off the top after thirteen weeks. Ed was back at number one the following week. Harry had played his friend the tracks from the album before it was released and ignored the fact that he had liked one particular song – it didn't make the final selection and Harry has never said what song it was. Ed had also offered him one of his own songs in the early days of writing the album – that wasn't chosen either.

Unusually, 'Sign of the Times' made number one before the video was released. In this case, it was used as another promotional tool for the album. Harry was featured on a blustery day on the scenic Isle of Skye, singing and soaring as a spirit on his way to heaven. He even walked on water. It's just Harry in the video and we don't realise he is suspended from a helicopter the whole time. The effect was immensely atmospheric and won many plaudits for the French director, Woodkid (Yoann Lemoine), including winning the BRIT Award for Best Video.

Harry flew back to Los Angeles for the launch of *Harry Styles*. The name did not feature on the front cover; instead, we see Harry's bare back and the back of his head as he splashes himself with water. The artwork was shot by the much sought-after, award-winning London-born photographer Harley Weir. She infused her work with a dream-like, erotic quality that perfectly suited Harry, who was styled for the pictures by Harry Lambert. This was photography as high art not jumping out of the bushes hoping to catch an unguarded moment.

Harley graduated from Central Saint Martins School of Art and Design with a BA in Fine Art in 2010. She taught herself photography with the goal of moving people with her images. She was soon in demand with magazines and leading fashion brands including Stella McCartney, Calvin Klein and Topshop. She has also been constant in using her work to support charities that mattered to her – something that Harry was about to do.

A second single, 'Sweet Creature', was made available for streaming and downloads. Again, he declined to say who it was about, although he did admit the ballad was specifically about one person. *Teen Vogue* observed that it might ruin the listening experience if we actually knew, although it was widely speculated that Kendall Jenner was his muse on this occasion. The magazine also described Harry as the 'king of the vague answers'.

The final push for the album was a week-long residency on *The Late Late Show* when he appeared every day with James Corden, culminating in his own Carpool Karaoke. They sang 'Sign of the Times', 'Sweet Creature', 'Hey Ya!' (the Outkast hip-hop party favourite) and 'Kiwi', a rock track from the album. The banter between the two friends was fun and natural, particularly when they sang 'Endless Love', the Diana Ross and Lionel Ritchie classic that Harry used to sing on his karaoke machine back in Holmes Chapel.

The highlight, though, was probably not the singing but Harry acting scenes from *Titanic* and *Notting Hill*, from which he delivered the famous Julia Roberts line, 'I'm just a girl, standing in front of a boy asking him to love her.'

Harry Styles debuted at number one on both sides of the Atlantic. The first-week sales in the US of 230,000 were the highest by a British male artist on debut. Globally it sold more than a million copies before the end of the year.

Generally, the critics were kind. They took the album seriously and not one to dismiss as a boy-band vanity project. The *NME* noted the debt to seventies and eighties classic rock, fusing together the Eagles, Elton John, Warren Zevon and Mötley Crüe. The Laurel Canyon sound of 'Sweet Creature' contrasted sharply with the 'Aerosmith stomp' of 'Kiwi'.

Variety observed that few people could have predicted that Harry would 'drop the kind of album that makes your uncle or mum perk up and say, "what's that?"'. The review also assessed the three defining themes of the record to be: 'Romance', 'lost love' and 'sex' – stating that even the 'sex is laced with sadness'.

Harry's use of dinosaur-rock lyrics to describe women was noticed. Roisin O'Connor, in the *Independent*, drew attention to lines such as she's a 'devil in between the sheets' and 'she's a good girl, such a good girl'. Giving Harry credit for his enlightened views on women she said, 'it's a shame he hasn't tried to break away from some of the more fatigued gender archetypes that dominate the rock music he clearly loves'.

He barely had time to enjoy his new house in Beverly Hills before he was flying back across the Atlantic for the premiere of *Dunkirk* but, first, the sad news that had been expected was announced. Robin Twist had died aged fifty-seven. Harry was very fond of his stepdad and the family asked for privacy as they grieved. Liam Payne tweeted, 'Harry my heart really goes out to you – such an extremely sad day for us all who knew Robin. What a kind, gentle and beautiful soul, a true rarity in today's world. Sometimes they really do take the best of us far too soon.'

Although Harry was now properly settled in Los Angeles, his family still came first. He dedicated *Harry Styles* in a simple, sweet way that said it all:

'To my family, I thank you every day for supporting me
And for loving me, H.'

17

RAINBOW

Six months before she met Harry, the chic and ultra-cool French-American model Camille Rowe was asked by a fashion magazine to name some of her favourite books. She suggested *The Master and Margarita* by the Russian novelist Mikhail Bulgakov, practically anything by Richard Brodhagen, author of *Finding God in Sin City*, and … *In Watermelon Sugar* by Richard Brautigan.

Camille was a passionate reader whose ambition away from the catwalk was to open a rare bookstore in Los Angeles that would be more like a community club where like-minded people could meet to chat and discuss literature. She would certainly have a willing participant in Harry Styles.

They were introduced at a fashion party in New York by mutual friend Alexa Chung, who seemed to know everyone. They were seen together for the first time having a dance at the Classic East Festival, at the Citi Field baseball stadium in Queens, when Fleetwood Mac was the headline act.

Camille was brought up mainly in Paris where her father, René Pourcheresse, owned a restaurant. Her mother, Darilyn

Rowe-Pourcheresse, was a model and dancer at the Cabaret Le Lido in the Champs Elysées. Their daughter came to modelling quite late, especially in comparison to Cara Delevingne and Kendall Jenner. She was already at university studying film when she was 'discovered' seated outside a café in the Le Marais district.

Her rise to prominence was rapid, fronting campaigns for Louis Vuitton, Chloé, Abercrombie & Fitch, and in particular Dior, for whom she was the face of new fragrance Poison Girl.

In 2016 she modelled in a Victoria's Secret show, as many of the women linked to Harry seemed to have done.

The same year, she was the Miss April cover girl in *Playboy*, six months after the magazine had announced it would no longer be publishing nude pictures. Camille styled herself for a series of photographs across fourteen pages wearing a combination of lingerie and her own clothes. *Highsnobiety*, the online lifestyle magazine, described the images as 'classy and sensual in equal measure', pointing out that they had a retro feel.

Camille was an enthusiastic advocate of feminism, participating in The Women's March through downtown LA the day after Donald Trump's inauguration. Across the country, millions of women and men took to the streets to protest against the values he represented. Harry was moved to tweet his support the following day: 'Yesterday was amazing. Unity and love. Always equal. H.' Camille had strong political views to impress upon Harry. When she was asked by *Elle* what she would do if she was invisible for the day, she replied, 'I'd go to the White House and punch President Trump.'

It's not surprising that she and Harry got along so well right from the start. They had so much to talk about: books and fashion, naturally, but also equal rights for everyone. Harry had already given his support for the HeForShe campaign. They also shared a devotion to yoga, both finding the time each day for a session of exercise and reflection that Camille said made her feel sane.

And they both had acting ambitions. Harry had just finished his first film while Camille, who had already appeared in a number of short films and videos, saw acting as a career path after her modelling days were over. They could swap stories about their first roles – Harry as Buzz Lightyear in *Chitty Chitty Bang Bang* in Holmes Chapel. Camille, aged twelve, was in a school production of Edmond Rostand's verse play *Chantecler*, in which all the characters are farmyard animals. She played a nasty hen.

The only less–desirable thing they had in common was no time. Harry was about to embark on his first solo tour. He warmed up for the year-long global marathon with a small gig at the world-famous Troubadour club on Santa Monica Boulevard in West Hollywood. Many of the greats had played there over the years, including Elton John, Bruce Springsteen, Joni Mitchell, Carole King and James Taylor.

Harry's gig was an unadvertised surprise only announced on the day, but he did manage to organise a special guest to join him on stage. He described it as one of the best nights ever when he told the crowd, 'In my entire life, I never thought I'd be able to say this. Please welcome to the stage, Stevie Nicks.' He had forged a great friendship with the iconic Fleetwood Mac singer since his gift of carrot cake two years earlier. He called her his 'queen of everything'.

Together they sang 'Two Ghosts' – described by Stevie as a

great song – the Fleetwood Mac seventies classic 'Landslide' and her song 'Leather and Lace', which she originally performed with the Eagles singer Don Henley. A welcome legacy from his One Direction days was that Harry was excellent at harmonies. Stevie had a commanding presence at the age of sixty-eight. Harry was so overcome with emotion at singing with his idol that he had to pause midway through the performance to take a moment to compose himself. When she left the stage, Harry slapped his face and declared, 'I am losing my shit in a cool way.'

The gig was an ideal start to his solo performing career. *Variety* found his melodies 'irresistible'. During the punchier numbers from the album, including 'Only Angel' and 'Kiwi', Harry was described as embodying the 'swagger of Jagger', which was not the first or last time he was compared to the Rolling Stone.

Harry gave the proceeds from the ticket sales to the charity Safe Place for Youth that had started up in Venice Beach in 2011 to provide food and shelter for homeless young people. He would go on to support a whole raft of good causes throughout his tour.

Live on Tour began in San Francisco in September 2017, then the following day continued down the coast to Los Angeles. Harry had deliberately chosen small venues to start with, moving on to larger arena dates in 2018. The eighty-nine concerts sold out in minutes or, in some cases, seconds. The final concert would be at the Forum in Inglewood the following July.

His musical director on tour was his friend Tom Hull, known professionally as Kid Harpoon. Tom, who was from

Chatham, in Kent, was a singer-songwriter in his own right but was best known for his work with Florence and the Machine, Jessie Ware and Calvin Harris. He had first met Harry in London but started working with him in Los Angeles, where he had set up his own studio, Harpoon House, in West Hollywood at the beginning of 2016.

Harry brought him in to help with two tracks on the first album, 'Sweet Creature' and 'Carolina', and was keen for them to work more closely together going forward. They had musical chemistry. They also shared the same management at Full Stop, where Jeffrey Azoff was now guiding Tom.

Although Tom was more than eleven years older, it was Harry who introduced his friend to the sounds of the seventies that so influenced him. For his part, Tom helped Harry put the set for the tour into a cohesive shape, encouraging him not to completely ignore One Direction as that was part of his musical heritage and the starting point for many of the fans who had bought tickets.

At his very first *Live on Tour* concert in the Masonic Auditorium, San Francisco, he picked up a gigantic rainbow flag that a fan had thrown on stage. The universal symbol of LGBTQ+ Pride would become a fixture on tour. Harry wrapped it around the microphone, then around himself and waved it constantly. He encouraged his spellbound audience to wave their own flags back at him. It became as much a part of his performance as the hand-crafted Gucci suit and Gibson electric guitar.

His support for all things Pride was neither something he had just thought of nor an affectation. In January 2015 he wrote, 'I study rainbows.' These three words were retweeted more than 350,000 times. During One Direction's concerts later that year in Vancouver and in Buffalo, New York, he wore the flag as a cape when the band sang 'Act My Age' from the *Four* album.

A year earlier, when they performed at the then-named Edward Jones Dome in St Louis, Missouri, during the *Where We Are* tour, he wore a jersey with the American footballer Michael Sam's number '96' on it. Harry was showing his support for Michael, who had made headlines for being the first openly gay athlete to be drafted in the NFL.

His opening act in San Francisco, throughout North America and onto Europe was the Californian electronic pop band Muna, a trio of women who identify as queer. Harry had invited them to tour with him after he fell in love with their acclaimed first album, *About U*, a thought-provoking and empowering work that dealt with issues including sexual assault and the emotional abuse of women.

One of the trio, Naomi McPherson, explained that they felt protected as a group of three, a 'little army', and as a result she didn't feel afraid to be herself: 'That makes me proud to be queer. That's the whole point of why we do this. We want a safe haven.' Camille Rowe would have approved of the t-shirts they were prone to wear on stage, declaring simply, 'Fuck Trump'.

They were stunned when Harry asked them to tour with him and they were totally unprepared for the experience and the visceral passion of his fans. Muna singer Katie Gavin observed, 'They pass out, overwhelmed by being in the same room as him.' Katie had graciously referred to Harry on stage during the first concert: 'Harry has built his career, his essence, on kindness,' she told the crowd. The mere mention of his name launched a thousand and more screams.

A fire alarm, triggered by theatrical smoke in Muna's act, threatened to cut short the evening before the man himself appeared to start the concert in quietish mood with 'Ever Since New York'. His debut album had just ten tracks on it so he needed to include some extra numbers, choosing his own compositions, 'Stockholm Syndrome' and 'Just a Little Bit of Your Heart', the song he wrote for Ariana Grande and one made more poignant after the bomb attack at her concert in Manchester just four months earlier. His choice of 'What Makes You Beautiful', arguably the most famous One Direction song, was bold but he made it more of a stomping anthem, described by one critic as an 'empowering, inclusive sing-along'. One of the encores was 'The Chain', a signature Fleetwood Mac song that often opened their gigs. 'Sign of the Times' was a fitting finale.

Right from the start, the mantra for the tour was 'Treat People with Kindness'. He had picked up a pin for his guitar strap that had the slogan written on it. The sentiment resonated with Harry, who had it emblazoned on t-shirts that fans could buy at this and subsequent concerts. He explained, 'I saw a lot of t-shirts around. I'd be driving or something and see someone in one and I started feeling like, "Oh, this is a bit of a thing."' It was more than just a thing. It was the basis for a huge charitable drive throughout the tour that raised more than $1.2 million for his chosen good causes.

Camille was in the audience the next night when the tour moved down the coast to the Greek Theatre in Griffith Park,

LA. She was dancing and laughing happily with a friend. Other old friends were in the audience as well, including Niall Horan, Oscar-winner Emma Stone – a great buddy of Taylor Swift – and Mick Fleetwood, who according to his band mate Stevie Nicks had 'kind of adopted Harry'. They had met during One Direction days when the drummer had taken his two thirteen-year-old girls to see the group in concert. He was under strict instructions from his daughters: 'Don't embarrass us. No dad dancing!' His stock rose, however, when he did a meet and greet with Harry and they realised their dad was a superstar as well. Mick and Harry would keep in touch, writing to each other from all corners of the world. Harry, it seemed, could make a friend in any situation and it didn't matter what age or gender they were.

Backstage, he also met one of his childhood heroes for the first time. He loved the country legend Shania Twain for her fashion and her music. He and his mum would sing along to her CD as Anne drove around the quiet lanes of Cheshire. Shania was impressed by Harry, too, particularly his breathtaking blue floral suit.

At the start of his set, Harry told the crowd, 'My job is to entertain you. Your job is to have as much fun as you possibly can.' The *LA Times* was appreciative: 'Styles' charm offensive could settle wars. He was made to be the frontman.'

After the concert, Camille and Harry went out for sushi – one of the advantages of playing a concert in your adopted home town was winding down in a favourite restaurant. Camille was now living in the trendy Beachwood Canyon suburb of LA but still hankered after the small out-of-the-way bistros that she had loved so much in Paris.

They had another relaxed dinner out at the weekend before he left for Nashville. This time they were photographed and the newspapers couldn't help notice that Harry was carrying her handbag. He was certainly carrying a bag that might have been hers, or might have been his, or might have been one they were sharing. The media hadn't quite caught on yet to Harry's relaxed approach to breaking masculine stereotypes.

He had some time in Nashville so he went to The Cave studios where Tyler Johnson was working. Mitch and Tom joined them to kill time and kick around some ideas. They spent all day working on the song that would become 'Watermelon Sugar'. It's not about or inspired by *In Watermelon Sugar*, but the title of Camille's favourite book was inside Harry's head. Perhaps she slipped a copy into his suitcase. She wasn't there with him because she was modelling at Paris Fashion Week.

The book itself is an account of life in a commune in the aftermath of the fall of a civilisation. Harry's song was about the start of a relationship: 'That initial euphoria of when you start seeing someone, or sleeping with someone, or being around someone and you have that excitement.'

The song took ages to come together – probably the longest time he had ever spent on the initial writing of a song, even though the chorus chant of 'watermelon sugar high' had the gang throwing their arms aloft in the studio all afternoon. Harry was quite pleased with their efforts at the time but, as he once admitted on the radio, he grew to hate it. There was no way that particular song was ever going to see the light of day.

After a flurry of American dates, the tour moved on to Europe in late October. One of the principal sports of fans seemed to be reporting sightings of Camille. She was everywhere. She was even seen in Cheshire before the two of them flew back to Los Angeles to celebrate New Year. He had a break between a concert in Tokyo at the beginning of December and resuming in Europe in March, when he would be playing bigger arena venues including the O2 in London.

His first official job of 2018 was mixing business with pleasure when he went to Radio City Music Hall for the annual pre-Grammys MusiCares Person of the Year night that recognised the philanthropic endeavours of famous musicians.

For the first time it was given to a group – his great friends, Fleetwood Mac. Harry and Stevie Nicks chatted backstage and he asked her if she was nervous. She was but she told him that 'those butterflies' are what make the magic on stage. Harry's job was to introduce them for their mini-concert that closed the evening. He joined them to sing harmonies on 'The Chain', naturally.

Live on Tour resumed at the St Jakobshalle in Basel, Switzerland. Harry had made the decision to support a local charity in most of the venues as he toured around Europe and, subsequently, the rest of the world. Part of the proceeds from ticket sales and the Treat People with Kindness merchandise would go to a carefully selected chosen cause.

In Basel, Copenhagen and Oslo, for instance, he supported organisations improving the lives of children with cancer. In Amsterdam, Madrid and Milan, projects involving the provision of food for the poorest members of society was the priority, while in Munich he backed an association that offered support for refugees. And in Los Angeles, he chose the TIME'S UP Legal Defense Fund that provided subsidised legal support for anyone who had suffered sexual harassment, assault or abuse in the workplace.

One of the charities to benefit in the UK was the We Love Manchester Emergency Fund, which was set up to assist those bereaved, injured or traumatised by the Manchester Arena bombing in 2017. Harry was still including 'Just a Little Bit of Your Heart' in the show, but elsewhere he had freshened up things. He now began with the powerful crowd pleaser 'Only Angel' and had added two songs that were written for the album but didn't make the final ten. 'Oh Anna' rocked along with a supremely catchy chorus and a homage midway to the iconic 'Faith' by George Michael. The second, 'Medicine', had a similar musical tone but an explicit lyric that prompted discussion about its bisexual links: 'The boys and the girls are here, I mess around with him and I'm OK with it.'

Camille-spotting continued around Europe. She was seen applauding next to Harry's mum at the Paris show at the AccorHotels Arena. A few days later, during his concert at the Ericsson Globe in Stockholm, Harry took a moment to address the fans: 'I love every single one of you: If you are black, if you are white, if you are gay, if you are straight, if you are transgender – whoever you are, whoever you want to be – I support you. I love every single one of you.' He was creating that safe place for everyone in the arena that night. His message to the fans as the tour had progressed had become more focused, much more than a pop star invitation to have fun.

That message of safety and kindness filtered through his performances, concert to concert. Back in the US, at the SAP Center in San Jose, California, he stopped the concert when one of the audience held up a sign that read, 'I'm gonna come out to my parents because of you.' Harry asked the young woman, who was called Grace, if he could read it out and asked her the name of her mother. It was Tina. He persuaded the entire crowd to shout out, 'Tina, she's gay!'

Grace, who identified as bisexual, agreed that Harry had created a caring environment for his fans: 'He is a proud supporter of the LGBTQ+ community and he's made a lot of fans feel comfortable and proud to be who they are and I'm just one example of that.'

His support for the community was evident in Philadelphia at the Wells Fargo Center when he noticed a fan, Karla, holding up a flag that declared 'Make America Gay Again', a riposte to President Trump's slogan 'Make America Great Again'. It was handed to Harry, who held it aloft to wild cheering.

Harry had been keen to emphasise that he was not a star making political statements but someone supporting what he called the 'fundamentals' of decent human behaviour. That philosophy did not stop him signing the petition supporting the March for Our Lives, the youth-led protest in Washington, DC and beyond demanding stricter gun control after the notorious Valentine's Day mass shooting at the Marjory Stoneman Douglas High School in Parkland, Florida in 2018. He tweeted that he had signed the petition and encouraged others to do the same.

He waved a Black Lives Matter flag in one hand and the rainbow flag in the other when he was on stage at the United

Center in Chicago. He did the same at Madison Square Garden in New York when he sang 'What Makes You Beautiful'.

The concerts took place during Pride month. He had started the month, June 2018, by announcing special limited editions of his 'Treat People with Kindness' t-shirts on which the words were spelled out in the rainbow colours. They would be available to buy online throughout the month with all the proceeds going to the educational charity GLSEN, which stood for Gay, Lesbian and Straight Education Network. The organisation championed inclusive and safe school environments.

Harry's support act for the second round of North American dates on *Live on Tour* was Kacey Musgraves, one of the foremost gay icons in modern country music. She was promoting her latest release, the critically acclaimed *Golden Hour*, which would go on to win the Grammy for Album of the Year.

One of the tracks on this album was called 'Rainbow', which she hoped would be an anthem for those facing adversity, particularly in the LGBTQ+ community. She dedicated the song to them, although it was a 'song for anybody with any kind of weight on their shoulders'.

At Madison Square Garden in New York, she came on stage in a stunning metallic rainbow-patterned dress for a duet with Harry of 'You're Still the One'. Harry confided to the audience that the song was a personal favourite. *US* magazine described his duet with Kacey as 'one of the biggest treats of the night'.

Live on Tour ended back in California where it had begun. On the last evening at The Forum, he stopped to chat with the audience. One girl from Rhode Island had been to see the show seven times from New York to LA. He then read out a sign that said 'I'm gay and I love you.' Harry said, 'I love you too,' before adding to huge cheers, 'We're all a little bit gay, aren't we?'

In ten months, he had performed in front of more than 800,000 fans, grossing more than $62 million dollars. He had told 20,000 of them in New York: 'There is just pure joy in this room.' That had been true of eighty-nine evenings and would be hard to top.

18

FEELING BLUE

———————

Harry was in the shower when Tom Hull popped round, so his friend and collaborator sat down at the piano and started tinkering with a few melodies. Harry heard him, came out dressed in a towel, grabbed a pen and notebook and started to sing along. They were supposed to be heading out, but this was more important. An hour later they had written the bones of 'Falling', one of the most moving songs on Harry's second album.

It was about Camille. Her relationship with Harry had not survived the end of *Live on Tour*. He was distressed about it, unused to a painful break-up that left him unhappy.

When the media realised that he and Camille had split, the lyrics of his new album were studied for any references to their relationship. 'Falling', it was thought, was a half-hidden reference to Harry being unfaithful. The most obvious link to Camille was in the mention of the coffee being out at the Beachwood café, the local eatery that was one of her favourite breakfast and brunch places.

The most obvious song about Camille is 'Cherry', which has nothing whatsoever to do with fruit. She is heard speaking on the track, which gives the game away. Cherry is probably a playful corruption of *cherie*, the affectionate French word for darling. The song is about jealousy and hurt. In the past Harry had spoken of his songs not being aimed at specific people but this one clearly is, especially apparent in the line, 'Does he take you walking round his parents' gallery?', which seems to be a reference to Camille's new boyfriend Theo Niarchos, one of the most prominent members of the art scene in Los Angeles.

Theo is a member of the famous Niarchos Greek shipping family and the son of billionaire Philip Niarchos, one of the most prominent collectors of art in the world. Theo owns the prestigious gallery 6817 Melrose in West Hollywood, and he and Camille have continued their relationship, described by *Tatler* as the art world's latest 'It-couple'.

'Cherry' was another song that grew from some dabbling around in the studio – on this occasion the famous Shangri-La studios in Malibu, owned by the famed record producer Rick Rubin. Both Adele and Ed Sheeran are among the artists who have recorded there. One evening, everyone had gone home except Tyler Johnson and Harry's chief engineer for the new album, Sammy Witte. Tyler had already given Harry the good advice of not forcing himself to compose big songs: 'You just have to make the record that you want to make right now. That's it.'

Sammy was toying with some riffs on the guitar and, as was the case with 'Falling', the song just grew from a simple beginning. The finishing touch was the sound of Camille's voice.

The lyrics very much reflect a bitter moment in time but Harry had recovered enough to ask Camille if it was alright to use a recorded message that she had left on his answer phone. She agreed and was happy with the result. Luckily, she had said 'Coucou', her familiar French hello greeting, in the perfect key.

Her words are just snatches of conversation spliced together and don't make any proper sense but they gave the melancholic song an atmosphere, especially as Harry had sung that he 'missed her accent'. The third mournful song on the new album was 'To Be So Lonely', in which he gives himself a hard time for being an arrogant man who finds it impossible to say sorry.

He had to move on. Camille had left a distinct impression on him; she had a sense of style he embraced, often wearing each other's clothes, and from being an occasional reader, he became an enthusiastic one. To begin with, he had followed her reading lead so as not to appear a 'dummy' but now he might spend a whole day devouring one book. That was the case with *Norwegian Wood*, the 1987 novel by the much-admired Japanese author Haruki Murakami. The sensitive and nostalgic tale of passion, sex and loss is triggered when the narrator hears a version of the famous Beatles song. It became a favourite book for Harry. When he was asked by *Rolling Stone* what his new album was about he replied, 'It's all about having sex and feeling sad.'

He had to get on and write the rest of the album. His Camille trilogy – 'Cherry', 'Falling' and 'To Be So Lonely' – would eventually be placed consecutively on the album and would have qualified Harry as an old-style singer-songwriter, but he had other plans for his new music. He was determined the album was not going to be a one-dimensional wail into his hankie.

Fortunately, there was no rush with the new material. He didn't have to record in his hotel bedroom while on tour. He spent two years writing and recording *Fine Line*. The idea for the title track was one that came very early on. During the break midway through *Live on Tour* he and Tom started out just strumming on a guitar and gradually the song took enough shape for him to take an early demo on tour with him. He was so pleased with it that every night he would listen to the song before bed. Harry always planned for it to close the album, as well as be the title track. He observed, 'It's one of those songs that I've always wanted to make.'

He only took two weeks off after the tour ended before he was immersed in the album. Any fans who were hoping that 'Medicine' or 'Oh Anna' would be included would be disappointed. 'Watermelon Sugar' returned, however. Harry had warmed to the song again, although it still wasn't his favourite – the two he liked most were 'Cherry' and 'Fine Line'.

The first of the new tracks was 'Golden', a perfect soft-rock car song for driving on a summer's day with the hood down. He was thinking of a trip along the Pacific Coast Highway in California. 'It feels so Malibu to me,' he said. The video filmed on the beautiful Amalfi coast in Italy featured Harry running, swimming and sitting behind the wheel of a vintage Alfa Romeo car.

While he was writing and recording *Fine Line*, two of the great classic albums were on his mind – *Astral Weeks* by Van Morrison and Joni Mitchell's *Blue*. Harry had written a song called 'Canyon Moon', which many fans thought referred to Beachwood Canyon where Camille lived. The song had a folk-rock theme and Harry decided to track down the dulcimer that featured on several of the tracks from *Blue*. That album, which also has a melancholic feel, included many songs that were inspired by a doomed relationship – this time between Joni and Graham Nash of Crosby, Stills and Nash. They had lived together in the Laurel Canyon area of LA for three years.

Harry found the maker of Joni's dulcimer, Joellen Lapidus, in Culver City just north of the city and bought one just like the instrument she had sold to Joni at the Big Sur Folk Festival in 1969. The ancient stringed instrument, akin to a zither, subsequently featured on this new track.

Eventually, Harry just needed one track to finish the album. He had been reluctant to write a song called 'Treat People with Kindness' in case it looked as if he was cashing in on a message that he believed in. He had mentioned the possibility to Jeff Bhasker, who encouraged him to just go ahead and get on with it. The result was like no other track on the album.

'TPWK', as it was often shortened to, was not a break-up song or a navel-gazer but an uplifting slice of choral musical theatre that might have featured in one of the popular stage shows of the sixties or early seventies – perhaps *Hair*, *Godspell* or *Jesus Christ Superstar*. Once again, he wasn't sure if he actually liked the song but he grew to embrace it.

It contained a simple but strong message. He explained, 'It's about being a lot nicer to each other than, "Don't do this, or don't do that, not this yes that." It's just saying "treat people with kindness".' He always felt it would be a showstopper when he toured *Fine Line*.

* * *

Harry cited Joni Mitchell when he spoke in honour of Stevie Nicks at the Barclays Center, in Brooklyn, in March 2019. Harry was the perfect choice to give the presentation speech when she became the first woman to be inducted twice into the Rock and Roll Hall of Fame. His speech was a tour de force: he was full of praise for her but was able to mix in some personal details at the same time.

He recalled how the classic 'Dreams' was the first song he knew all the words to before he knew what they meant. He thought the song was about the weather – 'Thunder only happens when it's raining' – and not about the agony of a relationship in turmoil, which was rather an apt subject for a song considering what he had gone through the previous year.

He told his audience that Stevie walked a path created by Joni and Janis Joplin – 'visionary women who had to throw a couple of elbows to create their own space'. He continued, 'If you're lucky enough to know her, she's always there for you,' and added, 'Her songs make you ache, feel on top of the world, make you want to dance, and usually all three at the same time. She's responsible for more running mascara – including my own – than all the bad dates in history combined.'

He then sang another duet with the star he idolised. This time it was her 1981 hit 'Stop Draggin' My Heart Around', which she originally sang with the late Tom Petty. Backstage, Stevie amusingly referred to Harry as a member of NSYNC – Justin Timberlake's boy band – although she quickly corrected herself. She was very complimentary and said, 'This beautiful child should've been born in 1948 too, because he just fits in with all of us.'

He was back in New York in May 2019 for one of the biggest events in his career to date. He attended the world-famous Met Gala – also known as the Met Ball – for the first time but he wasn't a guest, he was a co-chair. In just a few years he had progressed from sitting in the front row watching Cara Delevingne walk the runway to being the centre of attention himself at one of the fashion fundraising events of the year.

Celebrities and the leading names of fashion literally queue up at the Metropolitan Museum of Art (the Met) on Fifth Avenue to be seen. The permanent host each year is *Vogue's* Anna Wintour, who had been a great supporter of Harry since his earlier days at London Fashion Week. Alongside her are guest co-chairs that in the past had included such superstars as Rihanna, George Clooney and Justin Timberlake.

In 2019 her co-chairs were Lady Gaga, Serena Williams, Alessandro Michele and Harry, who would be the youngest ever star to accept her invitation. The theme for the evening was 'Camp: Notes on Fashion', inspired by the American writer Susan Sontag's groundbreaking 1964 essay of that name, which explored the history and connotations of 'camp' in culture through the ages.

This was camp as art, not as a saucy seaside postcard. Its importance as a genre was highlighted by Max Hollein, the Met's director, who explained that while it has often been trivialised, the exhibition 'will reveal its profound influence on both high art and popular culture'.

The theme was perfect for Harry, pushing back the boundaries of contemporary taste by blurring the traditional lines of gender. Anna said she was hoping that he would wear something that was 'daring and fearless and colourful and different'. He wore Gucci, of course, but his outfit turned out to be not at all colourful – he left that to Alessandro, who was in bright red.

Instead, Harry was dressed in a sheer black ruffled top with a lace bib, very high-waisted black trousers, patent leather boots and a single pearl-drop earring in his right ear. He also wore a number of Gucci rings on his fingers, including one that was the letter H and another a large S.

After the extravagant stage wear of *Live on Tour*, the look was a complete surprise – not a sequin in sight. Harry Lambert explained that they had decided to take traditionally feminine elements of fashion – the frills, the sheer fabric and the pearl earring – 'rephrasing' them as masculine pieces with high-waisted tailored trousers and the striking tattoos. He described the effect as 'elegant', adding, 'It's camp but still Harry.' Afterwards the fashion commentators concluded that Harry had 'won the night'.

For the Gucci after party, he changed into a white, billowing top with a large red bow tie that Harry Lambert said was homage to the New Romantic movement of the 1980s when Duran Duran and Spandau Ballet ruled the charts. Harry didn't wear Alessandro's designs exclusively but it seemed everyone thought he did, so it was a win–win arrangement for the fashion house.

Kendall Jenner was at the event, looking the epitome of glamorous fun as she paraded in a scarlet Versace creation of feathers that represented fire. Understandably, pictures of them happily chatting away went round the world. They were clearly still the best of friends. Like Harry, Kendall had a wonderful smile for the cameras when working but preferred to keep pictures of her with a significant other to a minimum. Since she was first linked to Harry, she has had a number of boyfriends, most of whom seemed to be very tall basketball players. She has been dating NBA star Devin Booker of the Phoenix Suns since early 2020. Devin, who won a gold medal with the USA team at the 2021 Tokyo Olympics, has a perfect middle name for dating a supermodel – it's Armani.

Kendall would be seeing more of Harry in Los Angeles later in the year when they were set to appear on *The Late Late Show*. Before that, he flew to London to take his mum and sister to the Fleetwood Mac concert at Wembley Stadium. They all posed with the band backstage.

Stevie addressed the crowd: 'I'd like to dedicate this to my little muse, Harry Styles, who brought his mother tonight. Her name is Anne; and I think you did a really good job of raising Harry, Anne, because he's really a gentleman, sweet and talented, and boy, that appeals to me.' Anne put her arms around the son she loved so much while Stevie sang 'Landslide'.

Behind closed doors, Harry and Jeffrey Azoff were having meetings with Rob Stringer to plan the strategy for turning *Fine Line* into the massive commercial success they felt it deserved to be. Rob doesn't have to take a personal interest in every artist but he had detected a 'uniqueness' in Harry and believed that he had an exciting musical future in front of him.

The attraction of Harry as a long-term star was that he wasn't constrained by the expected. Rob observed, 'There is nothing formulaic about him whatsoever.' Jeffrey echoed that view, praising Harry for delivering music that people didn't see coming. He famously described his client and friend as a 'unicorn', the legendary mythological creature that symbolises something rare, unique and precious.

In these meetings Harry was not some vague pop star nipping to the toilets for a line of coke – although he is happy to admit that magic mushrooms at the Shangri-La studios added enjoyably to the creative process of *Fine Line*. Instead, he is focused, business-like and brimming with ideas. He insisted, for instance, that 'Lights Up' should be the first single from the album.

The song could scarcely have been more different from 'Sign of the Times'. Instead of a six-minute musical odyssey, this was a throwback to more succinct pop times, when after a couple of minutes the DJ was lining up another track. 'Lights Up' was two minutes and fifty-two seconds.

The track was advertised mysteriously on billboards that declared simply, 'Do You Know Who You Are?' using the same teasing tactic that had worked so well for Adele with 'Hello'. The words were the last line of the song. In one tweet he even shortened it to just 'Do'.

Harry was quite enigmatic when he talked about the song, telling Roman Kemp on Capital Radio's breakfast show that it was about freedom: 'It's about self-reflection and self-discovery. It feels very free to me – a couple of things that I've thought about and I guess wrestled with a little bit over the last couple of years. It's kind of like accepting all of those things. It's a very positive song to me.'

In another interview, he told Hits Radio that the track was 'very liberating'. His words were seized upon as an indication that it was a bisexual anthem, especially as it was released on 11 October 2019 – National Coming Out Day. Harry didn't address the date specifically or in any personal way but it reflected his ongoing support for the LGBTQ+ community and the right to celebrate one's sexuality openly and safely.

Harry was expanding on the culture of acceptance that he promoted so strongly during the concerts of *Live on Tour* and with his mantra 'Treat People with Kindness'. He even started up a website called 'Do You Know Who You Are', in which a visitor could enter their name and receive a personal compliment from Harry to give them a boost. It was signed H and TPWK and was created for World Mental Health Day – another cause that Harry strongly supported. He even responded personally to a post from a fan who said she would skip therapy to come to his next tour. He told her: 'Go to therapy, it's important. I'll wait for you.' He had started counselling in Los Angeles while working on his first album and had found it to be of enormous help in addressing some personal issues. He was sceptical at first but subsequently advised his friends to go.

The video for 'Lights Up' also premiered on the day of its release. Harry had travelled to Cancun, Mexico, back in August for filming. The director was Californian, Vincent Haycock, who had made videos for Florence and the Machine, Calvin Harris and Lana Del Rey. He shot Harry bare-chested amongst a group of young men and women gently caressing each other and him. His torso was glistening, which he later revealed was down to liberal use of aloe vera.

In other shots, styled by Harry Lambert, he was riding on the back of a motorcycle and wearing some custom-made

Gucci as well as a design by a recent addition to his fashion circle, Harris Reed. The outfits caught the eye of the Harry Styles Fashion Archive, which ran a poll among its online followers to discover Harry's Best Look of the Year. The winner was the Met Gala ensemble but the Mexican designs were a close second.

Harris was at the forefront of gender-fluid culture. Originally from California, he was a student at Central Saint Martins when he met Harry through an introduction from Harry Lambert, who was the first person he had worked with in fashion and had acted as a mentor. It was Lambert who suggested he meet 'a person', without disclosing the star's identity.

The young designer made up a small portfolio of references – the modern way of describing examples – that revealed the influence of Bowie, Jagger and Jimi Hendrix in his early work. He went along to a *Live on Tour* concert at the Eventim Apollo in Hammersmith in late October 2017 to meet Harry Styles for the first time, battling his way through the horde of fainting fans at the stage door.

He found Harry very receptive to new ideas and someone who wanted to be involved throughout the process. While Harry loved his Gucci suits, he didn't want to be tied down to one look and would commission Harris to devise more informal, flowing outfits. All he had to work with for the 'Lights Up' video was a couple of swatches that showed the shade of blue Harry wanted. He had just three days to come up with the finished article, which in the old days might have been described as a sleeveless pant or trouser suit. Harry loved it.

Musically, 'Lights Up' was a perfect appetiser for the new album because it was authentically Harry and not so easily compared to Bowie, Jagger or Pink Floyd – as critics liked to do with his music. *NME* made one comparison, though, saying the track was less Fleetwood Mac and more Justin Timberlake. The *Guardian* suggested he had left behind the seventies' rock influence for 'more soulful territory'. The *Vulture* column in *New York* magazine called it 'well-tailored pop' and a 'breezy tune' but also discussed the lyrics: 'Styles doesn't owe us more than he wants to tell us, and it's not wise to assume that pop lyrics come from personal experience.'

Surprisingly, the track did not go to number one in the UK or the US, where it only reached number seventeen on the *Billboard* Hot 100. The video, however, has been viewed on YouTube more than 95 million times, so it was a job well done.

When 'Lights Up' was released, Harry received a text from his mum saying that she had played it to her dad, his beloved grandfather Brian, who had always been such a support. 'He likes it,' said Anne. 'He's just happy you're still working.'

19

THE PRICE OF FAME

Not everything was sweetness and light in Harry's world. He locked his bedroom door at night and made sure he had round-the-clock security. He had a stalker camped outside his Hampstead home for several months, a distressing situation that left him feeling 'scared' and 'very uncomfortable'.

Three days after celebrating the release of 'Lights Up', Harry was seated behind a screen at Hendon Magistrates Court in North London telling a district judge what had happened after he first saw a homeless man near his house earlier in the year.

Harry recalled, 'I thought it was sad that someone so young was sleeping rough at a bus stop when it was cold.' That evening, he stopped his car outside the bench, wound down his window and offered the man some money for a hotel room or some food at least.

Declining the money for religious reasons, the man, Pablo Tarazaga-Orero, asked for some edamame beans, which Harry thought an odd request, but he popped to a local vegan café to buy some sandwiches, a salad and muffins, and handed them to him on his return. It was the start of a nightmare three months that led to him eventually contacting the police.

His security team advised him not to interact with the man but the situation became worse. The court heard that Tarazaga-Orero would show up at Harry's local pub up to four times a week 'anywhere between a minute and two minutes after I arrived'. Harry said that he started to feel as though he was being followed.

During a run in Regent's Park, the man blocked his path and asked him for the money Harry had previously offered. When he was at his house in London, Harry would see his stalker nearly every day and receive notes from him. He even pushed almost £50 in coins through Harry's letterbox for some unexplained reason.

One local resident gave evidence of a conversation he had with the defendant: 'He said he is a soulmate of my neighbour, Harry Styles.' Tarazaga-Orero pleaded not guilty to the charge of harassment and claimed that Harry had propositioned him, offering him money to go to a hotel with him for 'some fun' – a version of events that Harry had to deny in court. The district judge Nigel Dean found the suggestion to be 'completely incredible'.

Judge Dean found Harry to be a 'reliable and credible' witness. He described Harry's actions: 'These were honest, well-intended, good intentions from somebody who was trying to help another for whom he felt sorry and who he thought was down on his luck.'

Sentencing the defendant the following week, he banned him from going within 250 metres of Harry, his home or business addresses or attending any concert or event where he was due to appear. He was ordered not to contact the singer directly or indirectly, or post about him on social media; he was also handed a twelve-month community order and told to complete a thirty-day rehabilitation requirement.

It was a very unfortunate sequence of events in Harry's life. He was an ardent campaigner for causes that would benefit society and here he was involved in a court case against a homeless man. Harry has made no comment about the matter but he asked the prosecutor, Katy Weiss, to make a statement in court. She said, 'I spoke to Mr Styles yesterday and he is adamant he wants the defendant to get help, although he doesn't want to see him again.'

Within Harry's own showbusiness circle, stalking was a widespread problem: Taylor Swift, Ariana Grande and Cara Delevingne having all faced this unpleasant side-effect of fame. The worst affected was Kendall Jenner, who has endured several stalkers including one who was deported back to Canada and another who was jailed. Harry remained highly sensitive and cautious about revealing exactly where he was living at any one time.

Harry had not invited any glossy magazine to photograph his New York home, for instance. He had bought a luxury apartment in Manhattan for more than £6 million in 2017 – another highly desirable property investment.

He was there in November to host an episode of *Saturday Night Live*, a testament to his growing status. He was able to sing 'Lights Up' as well as newly released promotional single 'Watermelon Sugar', but it was his appearance in a wide variety of sketches that signalled his arrival as an all-round star talent. He was very funny.

His appearance was a good way of promoting *Love on Tour*, which he announced would start at the Birmingham Arena on 15 April 2020. Initially he would play sixty-three dates but he planned to add shows in Australasia, Asia and South America.

Harry was the host of *SNL* two days before the tickets to his tour went on sale to the general public, so the timing was perfect. In the show, he acted in one rapid sketch after another, including playing an airline pilot, a Chihuahua, an over-the-hill vaudeville act and one half of an Icelandic couple at a childbirth class. He had some fun in the regular monologue spot, declaring that he was grown in a test tube by Simon Cowell.

The regular cast were very appreciative. Chris Redd said Harry had been 'dope all week'.

In Stevie Nicks fashion, comedian Cecily Strong did not hold back: 'Harry Styles is from another planet where the most beautiful and talented beings exist. He is magical and I think it's safe to say we were all enchanted and delighted.'

An intriguing side bar was the response to his performance of 'Watermelon Sugar', which on the night received more than a million online views. Perhaps the song deserved more intensive exposure than being used just as a promotional single.

Reviewing the show, pop culture site the A.V. Club observed, 'Styles was into it all night, clearly invested in furthering his fledgling acting career, while getting to show-case some above-average sketch comedy chops.'

The acting career would have to remain 'fledgling' for the foreseeable future. There was no time. He was in the running to play Prince Eric in the live-action version of Disney's *The Little Mermaid* and met with the director Rob Marshall, who he described as 'the most wonderful man'. Disappointingly, his tour commitments in 2020 meant that he could not commit to the long production schedule. He had also turned down the pop-star role in *Yesterday*, the Danny Boyle comedy written by Richard Curtis that was inspired by the music of The Beatles. Chris Martin also said no before Ed Sheeran was cast.

Harry did have the chance to show more of his comic touch when he stepped in to host *The Late Late Show* when James Corden left abruptly to be with his wife, Julia, who was about to give birth to their third child, Charlotte. Harry had little more than two hours to make a dash to the studio, but at least Ben Winston was there in his role of executive producer to make sure it all went smoothly.

The highlight was a game of 'Spill Your Guts or Fill Your Guts', which he played with Kendall Jenner. Harry could either answer an embarrassing question or eat a piece of disgusting food that would have left the contestants of *I'm a Celebrity … Get Me Out of Here!* gagging.

Kendall asked him which songs on his first album were about her. Just when you thought Harry was going to tell everyone, he popped a piece of cod sperm in his mouth. He also didn't want to be drawn on ranking the solo careers of his former One Direction band mates, opting instead for a delicious mouthful of water scorpion.

Such exposure was great promotion for *Fine Line*. The artwork for the new album was revealed five weeks ahead of the official release. This really was a work of art and not just a few matinee-idol pictures of Harry smiling winningly. The cover was unmistakably the work of acclaimed fashion photographer and filmmaker Tim Walker, especially his signature use of a fish-eye lens.

Tim is one of the artistic pioneers with whom Harry has always aspired to collaborate. His photography for *Vogue*, *W* magazine, *Another Man* and *Love* captures the essence of the model or performer. He doesn't just roll up, shoot a few reels and go to lunch. He carefully researches the passions of the artist, which explains why some of his best-known work has been with two of the most fascinating and innovative stars of modern popular culture, Kate Bush and Björk.

Brought up in rural Dorset, Tim had decided to follow a career in photography in the early nineties after spending a year as an intern in the archive of the legendary Cecil Beaton at the Condé Nast library in central London. His job, stuck in the basement day after day, was to catalogue the collection. Now, he too is featured in the permanent displays of the National Portrait Gallery and the Victoria & Albert Museum.

The *Guardian* described Tim's work as 'dreamily surreal', a fitting description of his photographs for *Fine Line* in which Harry was dressed in Gucci – bold pink trousers, white braces and a black hat, styled as usual by Harry Lambert – in a set designed by Tim's long-time collaborator Shona Heath. One shot received the most attention – 'the lone nude', as Harry described it. He wasn't dressed in Gucci but lying naked on a yellow floor, his legs across a giant model of a real heart with his right hand placed across his crotch.

He told Ellen DeGeneres how Tim had persuaded him to strip for just one frame: 'It was like, "those trousers aren't really working so let's try it without the trousers." And then he looked at me and I was like, "These pants aren't really working are they?" So that was how it worked out.' Unsurprisingly the nude picture became a media story everywhere, which only added to the hype surrounding the album.

Behind the scenes, helping to guide the whole process was Harry's creative director, Molly Hawkins – an unsung hero but a vital component of his success. Harry had a stylist, a designer or two, various photographers, but Molly was a constant, orchestrating the visual image he was seeking.

She had first become involved in the Harry Styles machine after she heard some of the then-unreleased tracks from his first album. Impressed, she simply texted his manager, Jeffrey Azoff, who she already knew. She recalled, 'I was like "Dude, let me meet Harry. I think we could do something really special."'

Molly was far from just starting out. Her father was the celebrated bass guitarist George Hawkins, Jr, who died in 2018. He had played on many of Fleetwood Mac's projects as well as the duet between Kenny Loggins and Stevie Nicks, 'Whenever I Call You "Friend"'.

Molly had been in the music business for ten years, first as a DJ, then as manager of American synth group Chairlift, before being based in London as creative director for the Young label (formerly Young Turks) where she met and subsequently married its founder, Caius Pawson. While there she worked with Mercury Prize winners the xx, and, according to her future husband, took the label's 'game to a whole new level'. In Harry's artistic small world, Tom Hull released his solo records on Young Turks, so Molly already knew him.

Working with Harry Styles would give her the chance to bring her ideas to a much bigger global audience. She would be unobtrusively at his side if he was making a video or on a fashion shoot. Ten years older than Harry, she was attracted to the romanticism he brought to modern culture: 'When I think about seeing Harry live as a fan, I try to remember how I felt about Leonardo DiCaprio when I was thirteen; And how as a young woman it was fucking awesome to see a man that was so romantic and unabashed.' They have become great friends. It was Molly who gave Harry a copy of Murakami's *Norwegian Wood*, because she thought every man should read it.

Molly was heavily involved in the promotional campaign for the second official single from the album, 'Adore You', which involved creating the fictional island of Eroda. It wasn't too difficult to work out that this was 'adore' spelled backwards. Critics described the slightly surreal video as whimsical. Filmed in atmospheric locations around Scotland, it featured Harry caring for a small fish that he found flapping helplessly on some rocks. One of Harry's co-writers on 'Adore You', Amy Allen, described it as 'totally a love song.'

All the publicity and meticulous planning that had preceded the release of *Fine Line* paid off in spectacular fashion when the album was a huge and immediate success, particularly in the US. For starters, its debut sales week of 393,000 was the largest by a solo UK male artist since Nielsen Music started tracking the data in 1991. It was sixth biggest-selling album of the year in the States after just seven days. Perhaps most impressively, Harry became the first UK male artist to debut at number one with his opening two albums.

The critics were generally positive about what they heard. The influential online music site *Pitchfork* said, 'The actual sound of *Fine Line* is incredible, and most songs have at least one great moment to grab hold of.' The upbeat review was slightly spoiled by the observation, 'Styles doesn't have the imagination of Bowie.'

Variety noticed the influence of Paul McCartney but also the Californian sound of Crosby, Stills & Nash. Commonly, most reviews looked to cite possible influence and comparable sounds from Pink Floyd to Frank Zappa, from Motown to Mark Ronson, and from Lorde to Bon Iver.

In the first week of release, Harry played the whole album in order from 'Golden' to 'Fine Line' at a one-off gig at The Forum, in Los Angeles. It was yet more publicity and an early run-through for the tour. He performed five songs in an extended encore that included just 'Sign of the Times' and 'Kiwi' from the first album. He also kept 'What Makes You Beautiful', was joined on stage by Stevie Nicks for 'Landslide' and, eccentrically, chose to sing McCartney's slightly cheesy 'Wonderful Christmastime' as his seasonal offering.

During Christmas week he slipped over to London for a secret gig at the Electric Ballroom in Camden Town. For once Stevie wasn't the guest. Instead, during the encore Harry introduced the multi-BRIT Award-winning artist Stormzy for a rendition of his rap 'Vossi Bop', in which Harry joined in from time to time, including on the line, 'Fuck the Government and fuck Boris (yeah)'. Stormzy called Harry 'a legend'.

It was an uplifting end to the year and, for Harry, 2020 promised to be even better. What could possibly go wrong?

* * *

On Valentine's Day, of all days, Harry was robbed at knifepoint by a group of men wearing hoodies who followed him while he was walking home down a quiet Hampstead street. He told the US radio host Howard Stern that he knew he was in trouble when he twice crossed the street to avoid them and they were still behind him.

They surrounded him. One asked him if he smoked weed and Harry said no. Then the man asked, 'What have you got on you?', so he handed over a wad of cash he had in his pocket. One of the men lifted his shirt to reveal a knife when Harry refused to give them his phone. He told Howard that his first thought was how 'annoying' it would be to lose everything on his phone – all the contacts, photos, videos and snatches of new songs. He even considered hurling it into the pond behind them, but instead he ran into the middle of the road when two cars approached with their headlights on. Then he sprinted back towards Hampstead Village, cursing the fact that he wasn't wearing trainers. Fortunately, the men didn't pursue him. Howard observed, 'You could have been stabbed.'

Harry reported the mugging to the police but the men were not found. The next evening he went for a walk locally, accompanied by friends, just to make sure the unpleasant incident wasn't going to ruin life in his home neighbourhood by making him feel unsafe – although he still had the night guard at his house.

There had been the grimmest news that day. The body of Caroline Flack had been discovered in her Stoke Newington flat. She had hanged herself. Harry didn't mention her at the BRITS three days later. He didn't have to. Instead, when he arrived on the red carpet at the O2 Arena he was wearing a discreet black ribbon in the lapel of his maroon Gucci suit. That was enough.

Caroline's career had soared since her romantic interlude with Harry back in 2011. She had been perfection when winning *Strictly Come Dancing* in 2014 and helped to turn *Love Island* into the most-watched programme on ITV2.

That all came tumbling down when the police were called to her home in December 2019 after her boyfriend, Lewis Burton, phoned 999 and reported that she had struck him while he slept. Despite the tennis player not wishing to pursue the matter, she was charged with assault. *Love Island* dropped her as presenter for the upcoming series. Although ITV always insisted the door was left open for her return, her career, she thought, was finished.

In an Instagram post that was published after her death, Caroline said, 'Within twenty-four hours my whole world and future was swept from under my feet and all the walls that I had taken so long to build around me, collapsed.' She added, 'I'm not thinking about how I'm going to get my career back. I'm thinking about how I'm going to get mine and my family's life back.'

An analysis by the *Guardian* revealed that there had been 387 stories about Caroline in the UK's national newspapers in the previous six months: 18 per cent were positive while a quarter of them were negative in tone. In the month she was charged, however, there were twice as many negative stories as positive ones.

Caroline took her own life the day after she learned the case against her was going ahead and that she would stand trial on 4 March. At the inquest into her death, the coroner Mary

Hassell concluded, 'I find the reason for her taking her own life was she now knew she was being prosecuted for sure and she knew she would face the media, press, publicity – it would all come down upon her.'

She added, 'Caroline had fluctuating mental ill health, she had struggles in the past. In spite of the fact she may have led – to some – a charmed life, actually the more famous she got, the more some of these difficulties increased – she had to deal with the media in a way most of us don't.'

Harry was never going to make a spontaneous comment about Caroline for use in the tabloid press. He might have something to say in the future to one of his trusted magazines but for the moment he kept his thoughts to himself.

Harry's mum Anne had tweeted that it was 'heartbreaking' when she learned of Caroline's death and posted a profoundly moving poem about the woman she had always liked:

'How must your heart ache
To feel so all alone ...'

She signed off her message to her 2.5 million followers, 'May you have found your peace @Caroline Flack.'

At the BRITs, Harry had added a badge to his suit during the evening that declared 'Treat People with Kindness'. Although it had been his mantra for quite a time, it was even more appropriate and touching now as it mirrored one of Caroline's final Instagram posts that read simply, 'In a world where you can be anything, be kind.'

Harry sang a moving version of 'Falling' at the award ceremony, sat next to his sister Gemma and, ever the professional, appeared in cheerful good humour when the host, Jack Whitehall, came over for a chat. The R&B star Lizzo was conveniently placed at the next table so that she and Harry could exchange some banter before she downed his glass of tequila in one. He had already performed a version of her song 'Juice' at the Electric Ballroom and on Radio 1's *Live Lounge*. He had also joined her on stage for a pre-Superbowl duet in Miami.

Any future collaboration would have to be put on hold, however. On 19 March 2020, California became the first US state to issue a stay-at-home order to combat the spread of Covid-19. Just a few days later Harry made the inevitable announcement that he was postponing *Love on Tour* until 2021. The big question now was one that all performers were facing at a difficult time: What on earth was he going to do for the rest of the year and beyond?

20

IN VOGUE

Five days after the shocking killing of George Floyd in May 2020, Harry posted a heartfelt message on Twitter that revealed his true feelings about the scourge of racism and his support of the subsequent Black Lives Matter protests sweeping across the United States and around the globe.

He kept it short but immensely powerful: 'I do things every day without fear because I am privileged and I am privileged every day because I am white.

'Being not racist is not enough, we must be anti-racist. Social change is enacted when a society mobilizes in solidarity with all of those protesting.'

More than 820,000 people liked his post, an indication of the reach of genuine superstars if they choose to address things that matter to them and the world. He had already shared a petition calling for the resignation and arrest of the Minneapolis police office Derek Chauvin, who suffocated George Floyd with his knee and was subsequently jailed for his murder. Harry also donated to funds set up to help post bail for organisers arrested during the nationwide protests and urged supporters to do the same.

Harry's anti-racist sentiments echoed those of his new friend Lizzo, who had moved to Minneapolis in 2011 and began her recording career there. She posted a video in which she said it was not the job of black people to educate white people about racism.

She urged white men and women to speak up: 'This is your daily reminder that as long as you stay silent, you are part of the problem. I know you're not racist but you have to be more than that, you have to be anti-racist.'

And Harry did actually stand 'in solidarity'. A few days later he took part in a peaceful Black Lives Matter protest through the streets of Hollywood, barely recognisable in a bandana mask, sunglasses and a dark hoodie. He also knelt with others who felt as he did while listening to a rousing speech and he was thoughtfully attentive when a black fan told him of her experiences being surrounded by a sea of white faces at One Direction concerts and his own solo shows. This was a weightier commitment than waving a flag around on stage.

In London his sister Gemma stressed in a post to her nearly four million followers that Black Lives Matter was not an issue or topic that went away just because it wasn't trending on Twitter.

These were sobering times. As well as the hurt and outrage triggered by the killing in Minnesota – and the belated recognition of other black citizens who had died in police custody – the death toll from Covid-19 in the US passed 100,000 the same week.

In the middle of such stressful news, 'Watermelon Sugar' was released at last as an official single – the fourth from *Fine Line*. At first, there was no indication that this was going to become his most famous song to date. The video, though, reminded everyone of sunnier days at just the right time. It had been filmed back in January on the beach in Malibu – close to where One Direction had shot 'What Makes You Beautiful'. Because it was made at the beginning of the year, the effect of social distancing had yet to come into play and the advertising slogan declared, 'this video is dedicated to touching'.

Perhaps it would have been more accurately dedicated to 'slurping', as various male and female models tucked into numerous slices of melon. They were totally full up and fed up with melon as they cavorted around the beach. One model remarked, 'I was just praying it didn't come across but I just felt so uncomfortable.'

For once Harry seemed overdressed as everyone else was semi-naked. He endeared himself by being courteous and thoughtful to the girls, respectful of the #MeToo and TIME'S UP sentiments that had swept through Hollywood. When one of the directors told him to play with the hair of American model Ephrata, he paused and asked her, 'Are you even cool with that? Is that okay? Are you comfortable with that?' Ephrata was bowled over by his consideration and called him the 'consent king'.

The directors were Bradley and Pablo, part of the London art scene so appreciated by Harry, who were carving out a reputation in Los Angeles. Bradley Bell and Pablo Jones-Soler met while studying graphic design at Chelsea College of Arts and Central Saint Martins in 2010, the same year that Harley Weir graduated. The start of the decade had been a golden period for innovative thinking in modern culture in London.

Bradley and Pablo quickly established themselves when they moved to Los Angeles and had already worked with Dua Lipa, Cardi B and Kanye West. They had been hoping to collaborate with Harry for some time and grabbed their chance, although to begin with they hadn't realised the song's sexual connotations.

They met with Harry and Molly Hawkins, who suggested two images they should have in their minds. The first was the actor Jack Nicholson eating a watermelon with one of his devilish grins and the second a photograph of Paul McCartney at a beach party in the sixties. Harry and Molly wanted a video that represented 'boys and girls and sexual pleasure'.

Bradley and Pablo discovered that Harry actually owned a watermelon farm in a secret location near Los Angeles and so, on the day before shooting, the two directors and other members of the crew, including make-up artists and set designers, met up to harvest wheelbarrows of melons.

The following day's filming was a great success but as the time neared to release the video they grew worried that the record company might not go ahead, fearing that it would be seen as insensitive in Covid times. The opposite seemed to be true, as the public warmed to a reminder of better days. Bradley and Pablo observed, 'It speaks to what everybody is missing right now – physical human touch and connection.'

Since *Fine Line*'s release there had been much speculation as to whether 'Watermelon Sugar' was about giving women oral sex. The video settled any doubts.

The track didn't race up the charts, but in August it finally became Harry's first number one single in the US. From now on he would be referred to as the 'Watermelon High' singer and not the 'Sign of the Times' or 'Adore You' singer. The video has been watched online more than 256 million times.

By the time the song reached the top Harry had decided that he should spend at least part of the rest of the year making a film; that would still be possible even if a concert was off the agenda. He had taken time to think during a summer road trip through France and Italy with his friend the artist Tomo Campbell.

Harry was a keen collector of the fashionable London-based artist, who was another member of his circle that was shaping modern culture in the capital. Tomo was also an alumnus of Central Saint Martins who secured his big break at his degree show in 2010 when the famous photographer Mario Testino bought one of his vivid canvases. Alexa Chung was a collector too.

Tomo was introduced to Harry by his wife Sam, who is the sister of the former One Direction make-up artist Lou Teasdale and founder of the trendy hair and beauty business BLEACH London. They are part of a Stoke Newington set that had included Caroline Flack.

Harry returned to Los Angeles and was staying as the temporary house guest of Mitch Rowland and Sarah Jones. He was looking for a movie role that would be completely different to *Dunkirk*. He found it when he was cast in the psychological thriller *Don't Worry Darling*, the second film directed by the actor Olivia Wilde, who was also represented by the Creative Artists Agency. Harry was brought in to replace the original star, Shia LaBeouf.

At the time it was reported that the controversial LaBeouf had dropped out due to 'scheduling difficulties' but it was later alleged that he had been fired by Olivia for his poor behaviour on set. Olivia did a 'little victory dance' when Harry agreed to step up.

She had quickly become one of the most sought-after directors in Hollywood after the success of her first feature, the 2019 multi-award-winning high school comedy *Booksmart*, which President Obama included in his list of movies of the year. Olivia originally gained attention as an actor for her role as Dr Remy 'Thirteen' Hadley in the hugely successful drama *House*, which starred Hugh Laurie as an unconventional medical genius.

Olivia is a prominent activist and feminist. She was born in New York and comes from an illustrious literary and artistic family. Her grandfather was the renowned communist journalist and writer Claud Cockburn; her father Alexander was the Washington, DC editor of *Harper's Bazaar*; while her mother, Leslie Cockburn, is an Emmy Award-winning investigative journalist and filmmaker. Together Olivia's parents produced the 1997 movie *The Peacemaker*, starring George Clooney and Nicole Kidman.

They lived in the well-to-do Georgetown district of Washington and she attended the Phillips Academy in Andover, Massachusetts, where Presidents George Bush Sr. and Jr. went to school – as well as Hollywood stars Jack Lemmon and Humphrey Bogart. Olivia studied acting at the prestigious Gaiety School of Acting in Dublin, which boasts Colin Farrell and Aidan Turner among its alumni. She has dual American and Irish nationality and, growing up, had spent many summers at the family home in County Waterford. She changed her professional name to Olivia Wilde in honour of the great Irish writer Oscar Wilde.

At the age of nineteen, she eloped with the photographer and filmmaker Tao Ruspoli, a member of an aristocratic Italian family, who was eight years her senior. They married on a school bus in Virginia with a couple of random witnesses and were together for eight years until divorcing in 2011.

By then, Olivia had become one of the best-known faces on American television, firstly through *The O.C.*, in which she played bisexual bad girl Alex Kelly, and then featuring in eighty-one episodes of *House*. After she finally left the show in 2012, she appeared in several films but, more importantly perhaps, she branched out into production, taking on some serious subjects including *Baseball in the Time of Cholera*, about an epidemic of the disease in Haiti, and the Emmy Award-winning *Body Team 12*, which told the stories of those responsible for collecting the dead bodies during the Ebola outbreak in Africa.

For her directorial breakthrough in *Booksmart* she called all the cast together for a read-through and encouraged each of them to raise their hand if they thought anything sounded inauthentic. She wanted that collective experience. She also had one unbreakable rule on set: 'No assholes allowed.' She mentioned no names when she expanded on her thoughts to *Variety*: 'It puts everybody on the same level,' she explained. 'I also noticed as an actress for years how the hierarchy of the set separated the actors from the crew in this strange way that serves no one.'

One of the actors who benefited from this approach on *Booksmart* was Jason Sudeikis, who played the school principal.

He had become a household name as part of the regular cast of *Saturday Night Live* before becoming an in-demand movie star through films including *Horrible Bosses* and *We're the Millers*. He featured in a comedy drama called *Drinking Buddies* in which Olivia had a starring role. They were an engaged couple by the time the film was released in 2013, and subsequently had two children together, Otis and Daisy.

Olivia was determined to bring up her children in a modern, caring way, speaking openly about her desire for her son to understand feminism: 'I want to promote the idea that the definition of feminism is equality and it is not difficult to teach children because they are born with that sensibility.' It's easy to see that she might find a kindred spirit in Harry Styles – and vice versa.

Her second directorial project, *Don't Worry Darling*, was going to be supremely stylistic and she and her Oscar-nominated costume designer Arianne Phillips were well aware of Harry's appreciation of fashion and style. A film set in the 1950s exhibiting all the retro glamour of an old Cary Grant movie was perfect for Harry, although he did have to start the day of each shoot with a tedious hour in make-up covering his tattoos. Nobody had mentioned that future treat when he was a regular at the Shamrock Social Club.

In the film, Harry plays the husband of British actor Florence Pugh, star of *Little Women* and *Black Widow*. She is a fifties housewife whose life begins to unravel as she suspects all is not as it seems in her utopian world. Harry was cast as her 'picture-perfect husband Jack, who loves her dearly but is hiding a dark secret from her'.

Harry was happy this time round to see a familiar face on set, the actor and former model Gemma Chan. She was a good friend of Cara Delevingne and had gone out with Jack Whitehall for several years. She was one of Harry's circle who would enjoy nights out in Soho House or the Groucho Club back in London. Her career had moved forward quickly since she had appeared in the hit comedy *Crazy Rich Asians*, although her starring role in the Marvel Studios' blockbuster *Eternals* was yet to be seen, the release having been postponed owing to Covid-19.

The set for *Don't Worry Darling* was a happy one, partly due to the atmosphere of mutual respect cultivated by Olivia. She praised Harry, in particular, for allowing a woman – Florence – to hold the spotlight. She explained, 'Most male actors don't want to play supporting roles in female-led films.'

The popular actor Chris Pine, who had the other important male role in the film, said of Harry, 'He is an absolute delight. He's one of the most professional people I've ever met: Couldn't be kinder, more gracious. I mean, really, I was stunned by this kid. He's off the charts cool.'

Filming for *Don't Worry Darling* took place in Los Angeles and Palm Springs and coincided with the demise of Olivia's relationship with Jason after eight years together. They never married.

A crew member tested positive for Covid-19 in November, which resulted in Harry, Florence, Olivia and the rest of the cast going into isolation for two weeks. By the time it was over, all anyone could talk about was Harry's sensational cover for *Vogue*. It was instantly iconic. Anna Wintour had personally asked Harry if he might like to be the first solo male featured on the front. He did not need to be asked twice.

The front cover courted both controversy and praise because he was wearing a sky-blue lace Gucci ballgown that reached to the floor and was matched with a black Gucci tuxedo jacket. He broke the internet. Victoria Famele in the American lifestyle and fashion magazine *HOLR* picked up the positive; she called being on the front cover of *Vogue* a 'lifetime achievement'. She said it was 'an honour that tells the world that you are the real deal, it helps show the world what you stand for and helps the world realize how beautiful it can be'.

Harry went on a six-day juice cleanse to be in the best possible shape for the images. He was pictured by the acclaimed Brooklyn-born photographer Tyler Mitchell, who had taken the portrait of Beyoncé the previous year, which had become one of the most famous *Vogue* covers of all time.

Tyler, who was brought up in Atlanta, was just twenty-three at the time and was the first African-American to shoot the front of *Vogue*. Tyler describes himself as a 'concerned' photographer embracing all forms of popular culture, much as Harry crosses the boundaries of many art forms. He would have approved of Tyler's sentiment that he wanted to show a younger generation that they can climb the ladder and do what he was doing as well.

All the usual gang seemed to be involved: Alessandro Michele, obviously, was one – although Harry was by no means wearing Gucci exclusively. He now had a more formal arrangement with the company. The previous year, for instance, he had become the face of Gucci's first unisex scent,

Mémoire d'une Odeur, which was designed to transcend both gender and time. Harry explained how perfume triggered memories – his mum had always worn one that smelled of jasmine and Roman candles: 'Anytime I smell it, I feel like a kid.'

Harry Lambert was on hand to assist *Vogue*'s esteemed fashion editor Camille Nickerson in styling Harry for the day's shoot at the picturesque Seven Sisters chalk cliffs on the East Sussex coast. Harry's sister Gemma joined them for the day and featured in a criss-crossed Chopova Lowena dress, sitting on a bench next to her brother in one of Tyler's photographs.

One of the most striking outfits was designed and made in six days by Harris Reed. He produced a hooped skirt on top of a well-tailored suit. Some commentators weren't sure whether it was technically a dress or a suit, which was exactly the point of a fluid design and reinforced Harry's position as a face of gender neutrality. Harris observed, 'Harry just really understands the way gender can be restrictive.'

Harry explained his philosophy in a fascinating read by Hamish Bowles that accompanied the fashion pictures. He explained to the writer the importance of breaking down the barriers in fashion between men and women because then you open the 'arena in which you can play'.

Probably the most enduring quote in *Vogue*, however, was not one made by his close circle of friends, fashionistas or style generals. It came from Olivia, before anyone realised there was a spark between the two. She said, 'To me, he's very modern and I hope that this brand of confidence that Harry has – truly devoid of any traces of toxic masculinity – is indicative of his generation and therefore the future of the world.'

Her quote went round the globe and back again. Unsurprisingly, not everyone online was supportive of Harry breaking boundaries, with one commentator insisting we needed to bring back manly men. Olivia responded, 'You're pathetic.'

Olivia had very strong views that connected with Harry's – particularly where feminism was concerned. She and Jason took part in the 2017 Women's March in Washington, DC after Trump's election, declaring afterwards, 'that was the most incredible crowd I've ever been lucky enough to be part of. WOW.' A year later she carried her little daughter in her arms at the Women's March in Los Angeles.

Like Harry, she would demonstrate her support for a cause by wearing a pin at an occasion where she knew she would be photographed. She had attached a small gold one supporting Planned Parenthood to the red floor-length Michael Kors dress she wore on the red carpet at the Radio City Music Hall in New York where the 2017 Tony Awards were being held.

Harry also actively supported Planned Parenthood, a non-profit organisation that provided important sexual and reproductive health care, sex education and information to millions of men and women around the world – including advice and counselling about abortion. He wore a t-shirt that declared 'Women Are Smarter', inspired by the Women's March, which could be purchased through a site that donated part of the proceeds to Planned Parenthood.

Olivia encouraged people to support the TIME'S UP Legal Fund at the beginning of 2018, declaring, 'Time's up on silence. Time's up on waiting. Time's up on tolerating discrimination, harassment and ambush.' Later in the year, Harry donated $42,000 to the fund from his *Live on Tour* profits.

They clearly thought alike on many issues and, after a day's filming in Palm Springs, they could discuss them over seafood. They are both pescatarian. Harry had given up meat altogether during his tour, inspired by some of the musicians who were vegan. Olivia had moved between a vegetarian and vegan diet for several years before deciding that eating fish had added health benefits.

During filming they had been able to keep their blossoming relationship secret by meeting up at either Jeffrey Azoff's house in the Hollywood Hills or at James Corden's luxurious home near Palm Springs. There were the occasional paparazzi shots that hinted they might be more than work friends but the question remained: when, if ever, would they go public?

21

LOVE ON TOUR

New Year's Day 2021 began with the release of a new video that was practically guaranteed to put a smile on your face, especially as it featured Phoebe Waller-Bridge and Harry, doing more choreographed dancing than he ever did in One Direction.

The black-and-white video to 'Treat People with Kindness' was three minutes of undiluted joy. The directors this time were Harry's great friends Ben and Gabe Turner, two of the partners of Fulwell 73.

Harry and Gabe had been to see Phoebe's famous show *Fleabag* at Wyndham's Theatre in the West End and thought it would be wonderful if she worked with them on a Harry Styles video. The next day Gabe was watching old dance videos from the twenties and thirties and texted Harry to suggest it. He texted back simply, 'Treat People with Kindness'.

He phoned up Phoebe to ask her, which you can do if you are Harry Styles, and she readily agreed. They had to put in the hours with renowned choreographer Paul Roberts, with whom Harry had worked many times. The idea was a dance sequence in the style of old musical stars such as Danny Kaye or Fred Astaire and Ginger Rogers, with just a hint of Busby Berkeley.

It was as if Harry and Phoebe had been dancing together for years. Dressed in vintage Hollywood-style matching white outfits, they literally put on a show and it would be no surprise if the video ended up an award winner. There had already been so many singles released from *Fine Line*, but it kept Harry's name in the spotlight.

A few days later, he was the centre of attention again when he was photographed for the first time with Olivia. They arrived together holding hands and wearing black masks at Jeffrey Azoff's wedding to his long-term partner Glenne Christiaansen at the San Ysidro ranch in the celebrity paradise of Montecito near Santa Barbara. Inevitably the gossip columns were fired up by a new celebrity couple. This time, the ten-year age gap was not a dominant issue.

Olivia didn't accompany him to the Grammys in mid-March, which avoided them being the story of the night. He began the entertainment with a performance of 'Watermelon Sugar' dressed in a leather suit and no shirt, accessorised by a green feather boa. He had been nominated for three awards: Best Music Video for 'Adore You', Best Pop Vocal Album for *Fine Line*; and the one he won – Best Pop Solo Performance for 'Watermelon Sugar'. It was his first Grammy.

His acceptance speech was gracious, thanking everyone including Jeffrey, Rob Stringer and his three co-writers – Tom, Tyler and Mitch, from the first session in Nashville when they wrote the song. Part of his speech had to be bleeped out when he spoke of the other nominees: 'All these songs are fucking massive,' he said without thinking.

After the ceremony he flew back to London where Olivia was staying with her children. Circumstances had worked out well. Jason was in the capital filming the second series of his hit comedy *Ted Lasso*, so it was timely that Harry had signed up to star in his third movie, *My Policeman*, which would also be set in the UK.

Again, this film was set in the 1950s, which at least meant he had a retro look already in place. The film is an adaptation of the 2012 novel by the Brighton-based author Bethan Roberts. She had been inspired by the real-life love affair between the iconic novelist E.M. Forster, author of *A Passage to India* and *Howards End*, and a young policeman.

Bethan explained, 'They were in love for thirty years, during a time when homosexuality was illegal, but they managed to negotiate a shared relationship with his wife. I took some of their stories and built *My Policeman* on that.'

The screenplay was adapted by the gay activist Ron Nyswaner, who has been responsible for bringing some compelling stories to the cinema, including the legal drama *Philadelphia* that starred Tom Hanks, who won an Oscar for his portrayal of a gay man living and dying with AIDS.

The director of *My Policeman*, Michael Grandage, is one of the best-known figures in UK theatre, acclaimed for his early work as artistic director of the Donmar Warehouse and more recently as head of the Michael Grandage Company, which has branched out into film.

Harry was cast as the policeman. The names are different from the real-life story and in the film his character is called

PC Tom Burgess. His wife, Marion, is played by Emma Corrin, who won a Golden Globe Award for her portrayal of Princess Diana in the Netflix classic *The Crown*.

Emma and Harry were already good friends, having met after one of his gigs. She tells the story of one evening when he agreed to look after her sweet cockapoo, Spencer, at his Hampstead house. She was having dinner at a local restaurant and halfway through the meal received a text from her distraught dog sitter: 'He won't stop farting. Is this normal?' Laughing, he told her later that he would not be helping out again.

Emma is also the only other celebrity client of Harry Lambert. She too is a wonderful blank canvas for a fashion designer, always bold enough to try something new. Her floor-length Pierrot-style Miu Miu gown with a frilled ruff was the fashion highlight of the Golden Globes at the Beverly Hilton in Los Angeles in March 2021. Lambert had devised a stunning series of red-carpet outfits for a promotional tour of *The Crown* but they were all put back in the wardrobe when Covid-19 caused a postponement.

After the filming of *My Policeman* had finished, Emma came out as queer and said she would now be using the she/they pronouns. Her co-star, meanwhile, had been keeping a very low profile with Olivia in London. They were seen having lunch together and once in a pub but that was about it. They were certainly not pictured with her children. As was usual with Harry, no one knew for sure where everyone was living – although he was in the habit of visiting a boutique coffee house in Hampstead.

Towards the end of filming, he slipped away from the set of *My Policeman* to go the BRITs at the O2. He seemed to pop up from nowhere to collect his award for British Single for 'Watermelon Sugar', having arrived too late to show off his eye-catching seventies-style Gucci suit with brown leather bag on the red carpet beforehand.

He managed to avoid using the F word in his acceptance speech, in which he thanked everyone politely, but he was a 'talking point 'afterwards in that he had a decidedly American twang to his voice, which became the subject of many articles and online comments after the show. Harry attracted the most post-show publicity without doing anything much more than saying thank you. He even managed to eclipse Taylor Swift winning Global Icon.

Coincidentally, Jason Sudeikis finished filming *Ted Lasso* shortly afterwards, at the beginning of June, and flew with Otis and Daisy back to New York to his home in Brooklyn – one he no longer shared with Olivia. She was free, therefore, to join Harry on a trip to Italy, where he was shooting the final scenes of *My Policeman* in Venice.

After that wrapped, they moved on to an idyllic romantic break on a yacht in Monte Argentario, in Tuscany. It would be the last chance for the two of them to get away before *Love on Tour* resumed in September at the MGM Grand Garden Arena in Las Vegas. This time round he would be spending the first three months of the tour in the US. Hopefully that would mean he would see something of Olivia, although she is expected to be busy directing her next project about an Olympic gymnast. She has also signed up for an acting role in the upcoming Brad Pitt film *Babylon*, which is rumoured to be about a fading Hollywood star at the end of the silent-movie era.

They returned to Los Angeles, renting a smart home in the very fashionable Los Feliz area of the city while Harry began rehearsals again for the tour. Their blossoming relationship is complicated by Olivia's commitment to her children and any future arrangements are quite rightly kept private behind closed doors. In reality, it's quite early days and Harry has remained completely discreet about his relationship with Olivia.

Just two weeks before the tour began in Las Vegas, Harry received some very sad news from England. His beloved grandfather, Brian, had died. His heartbroken mum, Anne, wrote a moving message on Instagram about her 'brave and courageous' dad: 'We love you totally and forever. Sleep sweetly, you beautiful man. Go be with Mum.' Harry said nothing publicly about the man who had been such a fixture in his life.

Love on Tour finally began on 4 September, seventeen months after the intended first night in Birmingham. It had been such a long time since the postponement that the concert seemed more like a greatest hits event than one supporting a newly released album. He began with 'Golden', the first track on *Fine Line*, and ended two hours later with 'Watermelon Sugar' and 'Kiwi'. He didn't disappoint fans hoping to hear his version of 'What Makes You Beautiful', nor those waiting to see him dance with a Pride flag.

Harry had already announced that audiences at his concerts should have proof of double vaccination. On the night he said on stage: 'I want to thank you guys for getting vaccinated or tested to be able to come here tonight. The staff on the entire *Love on Tour* team has done the same and we are all taking precautions we can to make sure these shows happen safely.

'I know things are a bit different, but in order to protect each other, I also ask that you do your part by keeping your masks on while in the building and during the shows. I've always found that you can tell the most about a person from their eyes anyway. Treat people with kindness. I love you all and I'll see you very very soon.'

Two questions needed answering. Would he be wearing something fabulous, and would Olivia be there? The answer to both was yes. Harry wore an all-Gucci ensemble of an open vest covered in a pink-sequinned fringe, matching pink wide-leg trousers, and no shirt, revealing his famous butterfly tattoo looking as good as ever. The Harry Styles Fashion Archive online described it as a 'banger of an outfit'.

Olivia, who looked elegant in a powder-blue pantsuit, was accompanied by Jeffrey Azoff. They stood to the side and she waved at fans who called out her name when they recognised her, even though she was wearing a mask. And she danced along with the rest of the crowd. It was a happy night, although it was disappointing that neither Gemma nor Anne could make the concert because of pandemic travel restrictions from the UK.

Despite Covid-19 disrupting so many hopes and expectations, Harry had managed to win his first Grammy, his second BRIT, had his first US number 1 single, been on the front cover of *Vogue*, made two feature films that will hopefully come to our screens in 2022 … and fallen in love. His mother, his sister, his father, his close-knit circle of loyal friends and lovers past and present will be waiting with keen anticipation to see what this gifted and very modern man will do next. And that goes for all of us.

LAST THOUGHTS

———

On 1 February 2019 a quiet, unassuming character sat reading and drinking tea in a Tokyo café. It was his twenty-fifth birthday and Harry Styles was relishing the opportunity to enjoy his own company.

He read unbothered for five hours, engrossed in *The Wind-Up Bird Chronicle* by Haruki Murakami, an author he loved and arguably the most famous modern-day Japanese novelist. The *Daily Telegraph* described it as 'labyrinthine and hallucinogenic' and listed the 1994 work as one of the ten best Asian novels of all time.

The teeming streets of Tokyo were the perfect place for Harry to be alone. He walked back to where he was staying, listening to music on his AirPods, absorbed in his own thoughts. He chose tracks by the late, great Bill Evans, one of the most influential of all jazz pianists and composers.

Evans died in 1980 aged just fifty-one, after too short a life that was blighted by cocaine and heroin abuse. His 'Peace Piece' (1959) is a supreme example of musical tranquillity and Harry had chosen it as the ringtone on his phone.

The world is a better place with the Evans piano soothing your ear. His light and lyrical touch was once described as the music that would be playing at the gates of Heaven. Media organisation NPR described him simply as 'a genius'.

So there you have the perfect recipe for a Harry Styles birthday – the words of Murakami and the chords of Bill Evans. It's not exactly rock and roll, is it? But then this is a complex, intelligent and empathetic man who critics and so-called experts are forever trying to categorise.

Harry spent five weeks in Japan at the start of 2019, creating memories and thoughts to take with him. He explained, 'I never travelled alone. I wanted to spend some time on my own. It was a quiet time for me, a time to reflect on things.'

He had much to reflect on, since, in effect, he had left home at the age of sixteen, never to return to live there. He was very young and potentially vulnerable in the celebrity world of partying, but instead of going off the rails in a mad whirl of sex, drugs and rock and roll, Harry forged long-standing friendships with a mainly older group of people who loved his company and in return would be loyal and supportive.

Musically, it was a slow start for the boys in One Direction. Niall Horan always had a guitar with him but that was about it. Everything was done for them under the guidance of the leading Swedish producers of the day. They were worked very hard by a series of Svengali businessmen who successfully plotted their world domination.

Gradually their individual talents and forceful personalities came to the fore. They were five very different men. Harry, as this book has suggested, was always destined to be a frontman but he took a little time to be confident in his own abilities. His songwriting contributions in the early days were relatively scarce, but in 'Stockholm Syndrome' and 'If I Could Fly' he wrote two of the most enduringly popular of the band's songs. He also composed 'Just a Little Bit of Your Heart' for Ariana Grande and joined forces with Meghan Trainor to write 'Someday', which she sang as a duet with Michael Bublé – not exactly as prolific as Ed Sheeran but a more than promising start.

By the time he became a solo artist, Harry was ready to take centre stage with a small band of producers and musicians who would become loyal friends as well as workmates. That's one of the positive things about Harry – he works best and most creatively with those he trusts and actively likes, such as Tom Hull and Mitch Rowland, his rock-geek guitarist who knew next to nothing about One Direction before they met.

Harry's musical ability took shape as his own experience of life developed. A sixteen-year-old boy from rural Cheshire can write about his first kiss or his maths homework but not so much about life, love and loss.

These three key components of a songwriter's staple subjects – not forgetting sex – affected Harry as he forged new relationships and friendships. It's no secret that he has written songs about Kendall Jenner or his ill-fated relationship with Camille Rowe. They ignited his lyrical creativity.

Without Covid-19 we might be already thinking of his third solo album and what musical direction he would be taking next. But there is plenty of mileage to be had with *Fine Line* as he at last takes *Love on Tour* around the world. One thing is already certain from the American concerts – he remains a supreme live performer with an ability to make a connection with an audience that few performers can match.

Music is just one aspect of Harry Styles, the artist. He now has fully justified his status as a fashion icon for the modern generation – blurring the lines of gender and just loving 'dressing up', as he used to call it as a boy when playing games with his mum and sister back home in Holmes Chapel.

Critics, including fashion experts, like to compare and contrast influences and styles. I asked fashion commentator Alison Jane Reed if Harry Styles was a leader of fashion or a follower of fashion. She replied neatly, 'That is a very interesting question.'

Great rock and pop stars of the past have paraded on stage in the most eye-catching and flamboyant costumes. It is entirely justified to look at David Bowie, Mick Jagger, Prince, Marc Bolan or Freddie Mercury and decide that Harry is following their example. It's easy to imagine him coming on stage at Hyde Park in 1969 – as Mick did – wearing his famous white dress over white flared trousers and white boots.

But, quite frankly, what these greatest of stars wore fifty years ago is of no consequence to a generation born since the turn of the century. Yes, fashion trends come and go, but for anyone under twenty, under thirty – or maybe even under forty – Harry is a trendsetter and a breath of fresh air. It's all new to this current young generation; it's exciting and relevant to who they are and aspire to be now – blurring the lines of gender and breaking down the barriers of toxic masculinity.

Alison Jane adds, 'Harry is using fashion to say whoever you want to be is fine. He is the poster boy for gender equality, the idea that boys can show a feminine side, and that is great.'

Harry keeps and cares for all his amazing outfits and it can only be a matter of time before there is a major retrospective of his fashion at the V&A Museum in London. The JW Anderson patchwork cardigan he wore to a rehearsal in February 2020 is already there. And then there is acting, which as yet does not rival the heights of music and fashion on Harry's CV. He has now made three films and is in a serious relationship with the acclaimed actor, director and feminist Olivia Wilde. He will make more films, as he seems to have a serious talent and others seem to enjoy working with him on set. He may bring a large entourage with him, but he doesn't bring a big ego.

In each of the three main areas of his creative world, Harry has joined forces with a select few people that he can trust and whose opinion he values. In the introduction to this book, 'First Impressions', I posed the question: who are the people that have helped Harry on the journey to become the man he is today?

The making of Harry as a modern man starts at home, where his mum Anne and his sister Gemma were a constant female presence in his life. He may not always have seen eye to eye with his elder sibling, but there was a mutual respect which still exists.

Anne and Gemma are compassionate women whose outlook on life hugely influenced Harry as he grew up. He may be modest about his academic achievements in comparison to Gemma, but he has a natural intelligence and inquisitiveness that has allowed him to absorb and respond to different aspects of culture as he has come across them – whether it's art, fashion, photography, literature, film or, of course, music.

Gemma is a gifted writer, a talent she uses to highlight the causes she believes in online and through social media. It is an ambition she shares with her brother. During Mental Health Awareness Month in June 2021, she wrote on her blog: 'Something I can do with my platform is to help amplify the voices of others.'

Harry embraces that ethic. Clearly they think as one on many issues. This year she chose and endorsed a series of products called Doing Good that included candles and room sprays that do not harm the planet. Part of the proceeds goes towards MQ Mental Health, a London-based charity for which she is an ambassador – perhaps it will be one that Harry supports through his *Love on Tour* when it finally reaches the UK.

Gemma has 5 million followers on Instagram and nearly 4 million on Twitter, so she really can influence online. Anne has 2.5 million on Instagram and in recent years has used her voice to tirelessly fundraise for Parkinson's UK, inspired by her dad Brian's illness. In October 2020, she raised more than £10,000 by undertaking a wing walk. She was strapped to the top of a biplane flying the Gloucestershire skies. 'It was a terrifying experience,' she said afterwards.

When Brian died in August 2021 the family asked for donations to the charity to honour his memory.

Through the early female influence of his mother and sister, Harry learned to mix easily with an older generation without ever becoming old before his time. He also appeared to have a sixth sense in choosing his friends wisely, favouring those who value their own privacy and are never likely to shout, 'Look at me; I'm a friend of Harry Styles.'

He is surrounded by a small circle of extraordinarily talented friends and influences that are at the coalface of popular culture, shaping the style and thinking of a new generation. Hopefully Harry can remember them all should he ever receive a lifetime achievement award, for he has quite ruthlessly ditched anyone who has spoken out of turn about him to the tabloid media.

He doesn't give interviews to the popular press, preferring to speak to trusted writers on *Rolling Stone, Vogue, GQ, Another Man* or a very few other publications who will produce a biographical feature that will be read and enjoyed for many years and not be tomorrow's fish-and-chip wrapper.

One of his go-to writers is the American journalist Rob Sheffield, a contributing editor for *Rolling Stone* whose 2007 autobiographical memoir *Love Is a Mix Tape: Life and Loss, One Song at a Time* remains a favourite book of Harry's. In it, Rob uses music to tell the story of his love for his wife, the writer Renee Crist, and how it helped him cope with her sudden death from a pulmonary embolism after six years of marriage.

The *Los Angeles Times* wrote, 'Sheffield is mourning another death as well – of the 90s, a decade of "peace, prosperity and freedom" when smart, creative musicians found a wide audience and women were encouraged to be visible and vocal.'

One can appreciate that an enlightened man such as Harry Styles would respond positively to such a lament. What makes him more interesting than the average run-of-the-mill icon is that he shares his private views – which have developed within his close circle of friends and loved ones – with a wider audience.

While his talents in all three key areas of his life have also matured – he is now a true Renaissance man – so have his views on the things that matter to his generation. They are not recent eureka moments. He supported HeForShe when he was twenty. At twenty-one he danced on stage with a rainbow flag during a One Direction concert, and at the age of twenty-four he backed the March for Our Lives. He was twenty-six when he took part in a peaceful Black Lives Matter protest in Los Angeles. And at the Ball Arena, Denver, on the second night of *Love on Tour* in September, he held a bisexual Pride flag that a fan had thrown on stage while he performed 'Treat People with Kindness'. He is still just twenty-seven.

So, I asked in the introduction what it actually means to be modern. For me, it is to represent the values that matter for a modern generation, not constricted by the 'good old days' and 'the way we were'. The modern generation thinks millennials are middle-aged!

The new generation – Generation Z, if you like – is sincere about racism, mental health, feminism and gender equality. This group responds positively to the genuine concerns of Harry Styles as he articulates his support in a way that isn't patronising.

His famous defence of his young girl fans perfectly encapsulates his absence of toxic masculinity: 'How can you say young girls don't get it?' he argued. 'They're our future. Our future doctors, lawyers, mothers, presidents, they kind of keep the world going.'

A Modern Man, indeed.

HARRY'S STARS

In Harry's birth chart, the Sun – symbol of identity and direction in life – is in the progressive, humanitarian sign of Aquarius. One expects a strong social conscience with this placement, along with independent thinking, a marked interest in the collective, and honesty. Harry's Sun ruler, Uranus, planet of originality, is joined to creative, visionary Neptune, which is the first of many indicators of Harry's gifts as a highly imaginative artist and star performer.

Mars and Venus, traditional symbols for masculinity and femininity, flank Harry's Sun, in a beguiling combination that gifts him with hypnotic attraction and universal appeal. This planetary combination suggests how important popularity is for Harry but, equally, that he is very courageous and that he can, albeit with enormous grace, resolutely push an agenda – one that at its core will be about embracing individuality, difference and the rebel.

It is impossible to ignore the sheer love of life that the tight link between Harry's Sun and Venus suggests. He values and deeply enjoys existence, is accepting and good at making

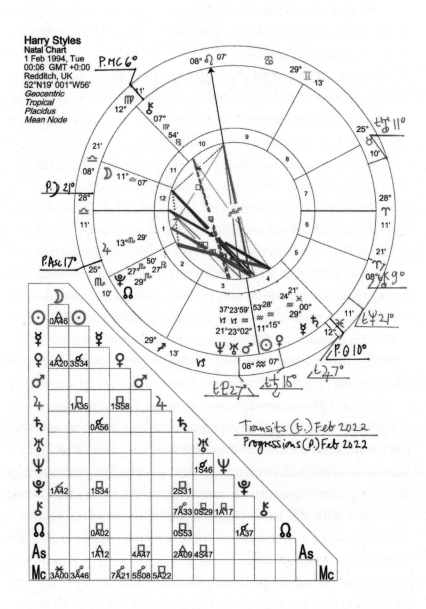

Harry Styles
Natal Chart
1 Feb 1994, Tue
00:06 GMT +0:00
Redditch, UK
52°N19' 001°W56'
Geocentric
Tropical
Placidus
Mean Node

Transits (t.) Feb 2022
Progressions (P.) Feb 2022

allowances, is instinctively diplomatic – with so much affection to give, has refinement and appreciation of beauty, and more. Does it matter then, if, thanks to competitive Mars, he always wants to come first?

There is a sense with this chart that the gifts Harry brings to the uncertainties and needs of our present times go beyond those of a shining entertainer. Here is someone who, through his craft, has gained a platform and has such enormous potential for contributing positively towards the balance of generational good. With his Sun and three other planets in revolutionary, egalitarian Aquarius, Harry will very consciously feel obligations to his world tribe and peer group.

He will also instinctively have the faith and vision that can move mountains. A strong link from the Sun to unbounded Jupiter hints at magnetic success and control over his destiny, but with a caveat: there may be times when his goals could run away from him. His sense of identity, then, could suffer – from unrestrained optimism and limitless agendas either of his own making or the design of others. And of this he must be careful. Like many of our leaders and idols, Harry will carry the projection of our hopes and expectations and, knowing this, he may feel harder hit by any failure to deliver. But deliver he will, giving back and paying forward, helping in the moment, because he can, with his Aquarian Sun being so at ease with the issues and zeitgeist of our times.

There is just a hint that when very young Harry may have been a shy communicator, finding it hard to express opinions, sometimes struggling to think positively and clearly – perhaps an older sibling expressed what he thought for him? However, as an adult – and partly because he will feel driven by just causes – Harry will become an assured, charismatic and genuine voice of authority.

Expansive, restless Jupiter, ruler of adventurers and seekers, is the planet that reveals much about Harry's initial education. It suggests that from early years he needed to test his faith and confidence in life and the classroom would sometimes have felt too small. Jupiter's urge for growth is amplified by the influence of obsessive Pluto, a sure sign that Harry would have strong instincts to evolve, to be rid of his old self and experience renewal. This is an ambitious signature, one of someone who needs a bigger stage, far away from the comfort zone of immediate community, neighbours and siblings.

These groups *are* important to him – he will feel the debt of brotherhood and positive experiences but he will want to respect this by following his destiny and then returning with the trophies of wisdom. There is, in the chart, a slightly Promethean feel, revealed by the melding of the energies of Uranus, Neptune and Saturn. Harry may bring a rebellious creativity and innovative mindset to issues of spirituality and our common values. There will be an instinct for finding peace and peaceful solutions, driven by appreciation of the sheer value of living in harmony and fear of the wasteland of negativity and hate. Few mediums are more suited to endorsing the concept that we are all part of one world than music, but Harry will be a role model in bringing that notion home, in making an abstract concept feel more real and attainable.

Despite the stellar trajectory of Harry's career – the glamour, the spotlights, the wealth, the recognition and the leadership credentials this provides – Harry's Sun position, at the bottom of his chart, tell us that home life and family will always be of fundamental importance to him. His background and his family circle are what provide both his confidence and sense of self, and he will need the security of a base far more than most.

Harry's love of his parents is a given – no matter if they disappoint – together with respect for his upbringing, the traditions and his personal history that have made him the man he is. He will spend a lifetime working through the issues that were created and thrown up in his early developmental years. These issues include fairness – whose voice gets heard, the rights of the individual over the needs of the group, who leads and how to manage the emotional fallout from members who no longer fit the team and his ability to move on from them.

For Harry, the Sun in progressive air sign Aquarius indicates a modern, collective family structure within which everyone pulled together but that also places a high value on each individual's freedom. There would have been unpredictability built into the very foundation of this unit because rationality, honesty and ambition would have prevailed as standard over the need for emotional passion or intimacy. The very close and very positive link between the luminaries the Sun and the Moon – representing father and mother – indicate parents who could easily express their feelings in a logical and tolerant manner and act considerately both to each other and their children. Thus when the group was placed under pressure, the default would be a civilised and intelligent split, with minimal conflict between the past, symbolised by the Moon, and the future, embodied by the Sun.

But such changes will have come at a cost to sensitive Harry – his conciliatory Libran Moon revealing through its position the pain of trying to keep his loved ones together.

A link between Harry's Libra Moon and dynamic Mars highlights the protective nature of his mother. She is somebody with an instinctive need to help others and will enjoy a challenge, quickly recognising opportunity when it comes. With her grace, ability to motivate and highly developed social skills, she will be more comfortable within a partnership than living on her own, and she has the skills to constructively turn around difficult situations. Mother may have side-stepped facing awkward emotional demands in favour of a placatory smoothing of the waters.

The father in Harry's chart is shown by the independent Aquarian Sun and Saturn in escapist, idealistic Pisces. Both placements signal absence but also duty and sensitivity. The father perhaps struggled with the commitment to satisfy other people's needs before his own but may have ultimately accepted responsibility and was supportive, embodying authority and vulnerability at the same time. A tight link between Saturn and intense Pluto hints at a degree of defensiveness and inflexibility that could be a block to emotional closeness.

No matter the fairness and kindness modelled by parents at challenging times, no matter the consistent loyalty and affection, there are indications in Harry's chart that it is hard for him to reveal his feelings and articulate his emotional needs. Harry has learnt that charm will take him a long way; his identity is very strongly tied up with being liked – he is compassionate and a people-pleaser and thus may shy away from revealing any emotions that seem ugly. As a result, anger and discord will be repressed or projected.

A great deal of Harry's determined and ambitious character can be traced back to his sibling connections. The linking of competitive Mars and rebellious Uranus shows how from his earliest days he would learn how to retain his individuality within the group. He would do this partly by fighting (probably with charm) for access to the parent, which is excellent training for navigating group workplace situations where he needs to lead and come out on top. A combination of authoritative Saturn and the youth symbol Mercury suggests a sibling filling the void for an absent parent and reinforces that sense of his need to push for recognition as the best. Often, these drives lessen the sense of connectedness to brothers and sisters, but they are beneficial for becoming self-reliant in adult relationships – sometimes too much so. Harry is highly focused and self-contained and may find it hard to depend upon others.

Harry's need for security will make it very important to found a home base or family group at some point because it is really only when he feels safe and able to express his deeper emotions that he functions at his best. Then there will be some sort of re-balancing towards a different ideal, one where he can live with a foundation of openly expressed emotional truth. The challenging connection between Saturn and Pluto suggests this will always feel dangerous until he has learnt how to be comfortable with acknowledging and stating what he really wants rather than what he feels others want him to be.

As far as relationships go, much of his life's purpose will centre upon his links with others – whether personal or professional – learning how he uses his considerable power and the journey of working out his own values for intimacy. In one-to-one partnerships Harry enjoys the fun, excitement, the glamour and unpredictability of romance, but the shadow of Saturn colours his Mars, suggesting his ability to trust others will be hard-won. He may be cautious about initiating flings and happier if others come to him. Then he might experience a clash between enjoying his relationships and pursuing his goals. Harry has very strong personal defences and part of him will remain alone in the midst of the crowd. He has enormous empathy, but in order for this to flow he needs to feel safe and able to withdraw, to be confident he will not feel trapped and that the privacy he needs to be creative will not be invaded.

In the run-up to Harry's Saturn Return, which occurs in March 2023, he will experience significant changes in his relationships. Pluto, symbol of death, resurrection and irrevocable change, first links positively to his natal Pluto and then contacts his Ascendant in a more challenging manner. Initially he will be drawn towards a greater understanding of his own psychology, the strengths and impediments of character. This may be prompted through a profoundly stabilising appreciation that his self-made resources are more than adequate to provide for his own needs and any important projects to which he would like to commit. His sense of identity will be supported by this to the extent that he will be prepared to take more risks. He will probe his values, able to prioritise the altruistic and intimacy goals that he can see will promote his own creative and spiritual growth.

Harry has reached a point where he is ready for change, allowing certain aspects of himself – perhaps illusions of control – to die. One of the spiritual laws that he will encounter is the Law of Abundance, which dictates that we must not hold on to things – he must willingly let things go, to let energy flow and trust this process of release and return. It is a period in which he must fearlessly confront the possibility of crisis and change. Relationships that have outlived their usefulness will go, and new ones, which have a more constructive purpose, will form. Harry can expect power struggles now and must be careful not to act ruthlessly or feel his ends justify any means. Challenges will uncover his weaknesses, but he will learn how to deal with them.

This clearing out precedes the return of Saturn to the place it occupied at Harry's birth twenty-nine years previously. Where he has undertaken the burdens and restrictions that life has imposed upon him responsibly and well, there will be evidence of gratifying, solid success. In the areas he may have neglected or from which he sought to escape, he may have some regrets. Aspects of life that have been tolerated, but are not truly where his energies need to be, will probably fall away. This sounds a little bleak, except that Harry's natal Saturn positively links to his Ascendant and Descendant – the relationship axis. Thus we may predict that Harry will find himself in the company of a group of people, or a significant person, or experience events that will play a profoundly important and positive role in shaping his destiny.

Madeleine Moore
September 2021

LIFE AND TIMES

1 Feb 1994: Harry Edward Styles is born in the Alexandra Hospital, Redditch. He has a sister, Gemma, who is three, and they live with their mum Anne and dad Des, a financial consultant, in Evesham, Worcestershire.

March 1996: The Styles family move to the Cheshire village of Holmes Chapel, twenty miles south of Manchester. Harry would go to school in this rural setting until he is sixteen.

Sept 1998: Moves from nursery, Happy Days, to the Hermitage Primary School. He is a boisterous little boy who makes friends easily – with both boys and girls. 'I wasn't one of those boys who thought girls were smelly,' he said.

Dec 2000: In the school's Christmas musical, he plays the title character of Barney, a church mouse. He recalls, 'I like to think I was a good church mouse.' He would also appear in productions of *Chitty Chitty Bang Bang*, playing Buzz Lightyear, and *Joseph and the Amazing Technicolor Dreamcoat*, as the Pharoah who performed a song in the style of Elvis.

Nov 2002: Harry and Gemma move to the Antrobus Arms near Northwich when Anne and her new partner, a publican called John Cox, take over the popular pub. She and Des had split when Harry was seven.

April 2003: Anne and John marry at a local golf and country club. She is still Anne Cox when Harry becomes famous, even though she and John are divorced and she and the children have moved back to Holmes Chapel.

Sept 2005: Starts at Holmes Chapel Comprehensive where one of his best buddies is Will Sweeny, son of Yvette Fielding, the host of TV's *Most Haunted*, which also featured her second husband, Karl Beattie. Harry is a regular visitor after school, scoffing pizza and chips in the kitchen with her son.

June 2009: Will persuades Harry to join his band White Eskimo with other friends Nick Clough and Haydn Morris. At the end of Year 10 they win Holmes Chapel Comprehensive's first Battle of the Bands. They perform 'Summer of '69' and 'Are You Gonna Be My Girl'. Adult tickets are £5 each.

April 2010: Skives off school to attend the first audition for *The X Factor* at Old Trafford, Manchester. His mum had filled out an application form for him and sent it off. Will joins him for the day and they queue up for more than five hours. Harry subsequently learns he is through to the first televised audition.

June 2010: White Eskimo play their biggest gig so far, at a wedding in the nearby town of Sandbach. They are paid £400.

July 2010: Sings Stevie Wonder's 'Isn't She Lovely' in front of Simon Cowell, Nicole Scherzinger and Louis Walsh, who gives him a thumbs-down. He is rescued by the other two. Simon tells him, 'You could actually be very good.' At Bootcamp, Simon warns there are no second chances. He gives five boys, including Harry, a second chance. Harry sinks to his knees in delight.

Sept 2010: The five teenage boys – Liam, Louis, Niall, Zayn and Harry – settle on One Direction as their name; Harry's idea. They perform 'Torn' at Judges' Houses for Simon and Sinitta and win through to the live finals at the Fountain Studios, Wembley.

Oct 2010: Harry suffers an acute attack of nerves before the band are due to perform 'My Life Would Suck Without You' by Kelly Clarkson. He is anxious he would sing the wrong note, but all is well on the night. Simon finds Harry charming and the easiest member of the group to talk to.

Dec 2010: The band tops the UK charts for the first time when they join the other contestants for the Comic Relief charity record, David Bowie's iconic 'Heroes'. For the grand final weekend, One Direction perform 'She's the One', with Robbie Williams joining them on stage. They finish third behind Matt Cardle and Rebecca Ferguson. Simon signs 1D to a recording contract.

Jan 2011: Harry and the boys visit Los Angeles for the first time, where they meet record producers and he buys lots of Abercrombie & Fitch t-shirts from their flagship store. They are greeted by hundreds of excited fans when they land back at Heathrow.

Feb 2011: One Direction perform five songs as part of *The X Factor* annual tour. When it finishes in April, Harry moves into a flat in North London, which he shares with Louis Tomlinson.

Aug 2011: Their first video is released to promote debut single 'What Makes You Beautiful'. They are filmed frolicking on a beach in Malibu. Harry splashes around and serenades model Madison McMillin. The video has been watched 1.2 billion times. Harry tells the official *X Factor* website that Caroline Flack is 'gorgeous'.

Sept 2011: 'What Makes You Beautiful' is number one in the UK. It would sell more than seven million copies worldwide.

Dec 2011: Harry is photographed leaving Caroline Flack's North London home on a wintry morning. Caroline would face a barrage of newspaper criticism about the age gap as well as online abuse and death threats. One Direction's *Up All Night* tour begins at the Watford Colosseum. He posts a tweet just before Christmas: 'Work hard, play hard, be kind.'

Jan 2012: Harry posts on Twitter following his break-up with Caroline: 'Please know I didn't "dump" Caroline. This was a mutual decision. She is one of the kindest, sweetest people I know. Please respect that.'

Feb 2012: On his eighteenth birthday, in Los Angeles, Harry gets his first tattoo – the outline of a five-pointed star on the inside of his left bicep. 'What Makes You Beautiful' wins Best British Single at the BRITs. He quietly moves in with Ben Winston and his wife Meredith in Hampstead Garden Suburb while his new house nearby is being renovated. He would stay more than eighteen months.

March 2012: Meets Taylor Swift for the first time backstage at the Nickelodeon Kids' Choice Awards in LA. She apparently told Justin Bieber that she thought Harry was hot.

Dec 2012: Taylor and Harry are photographed together walking hand in hand in Central Park, New York. She is also pictured with him on a break in Cheshire, the Lake District and in a pub near Sheffield, where Harry's sister attends Hallam University. One Direction's second album *Take Me Home* tops a million sales in the US. His mum gives him a belly button brush for Christmas.

Jan 2013: Splits with Taylor after reportedly having a big bust-up on holiday in the British Virgin Islands.

Feb 2013: One Direction wins the Global Success Award at the BRITs. They perform their Comic Relief single 'One Way or Another (Teenage Kicks)'. Harry is moved to tears when they visit Ghana and makes a series of video diaries highlighting the country's poverty and the need for improved medical facilities.

June 2013: Harry is best man at the wedding of his mother in Congleton, Cheshire, to local businessman Robin Twist, with whom he has a great relationship.

Sept 2013: Beams with pride at his sister's university graduation with First Class Honours. He tweets: 'She's all clever and that.' Harry is the centre of attention at London Fashion Week, especially when he is seen supporting the supermodel Cara Delevingne at the Burberry Prorsum Show.

Nov 2013: The marathon *Take Me Home* tour ends in Japan after 123 shows and a box office gross of $114 million. Third album, *Midnight Memories*, is released and again tops charts in the UK and US. Most of the album had been written and recorded in makeshift studios in their bedrooms on tour. He is photographed leaving a Hollywood restaurant with Kendall Jenner.

Dec 2013: Harry is crowned the winner of the British Style Award at the British Fashion Awards. He wins a High Court order preventing certain paparazzi from harassing him.

April 2014: Poses happily with fans after arriving in a Porsche for rehearsals at a disused aircraft hangar near Bedford. The all-stadium *Where We Are* tour begins in Bogotá, Colombia.

Sept 2014: Posts a picture online of himself holding a sign that declares HeForShe. Underneath he writes: 'I'm support-ing @UN Women and @EmWatson in HeForShe: As should you.' The post is liked nearly half a million times.

Nov 2014: Seems subdued at the recording of Band Aid 30 in Notting Hill. Rumours start that One Direction are on the verge of splitting up. Proceeds of this number-one version go towards fighting ebola in Africa. *Four* is released and they become the first band to have their first four albums debut at number one in the US.

Feb 2015: Turns twenty-one with a glamorous party at Lola's in Hollywood with guests including Harry's gang: James Corden, Kendall Jenner, Cara Delevingne, Rita Ora, Kelly Osbourne, David Beckham and the man who would soon be his manager, Jeffrey Azoff. None of One Direction attends but he is thrilled when Adele gives him a signed copy of *21* with the message: 'I did some pretty cool stuff when I was twenty-one. Good luck!'

March 2015: Zayn Malik leaves the band. An official state-ment says he wants some 'private time out of the spotlight'. He would later say that he thought One Direction's music was as 'generic as fuck' and that he and Harry had never really spoken to each other.

Aug 2015: After a concert at Soldier Field, Chicago, news leaks that they would be taking a break when the current tour ends.

Sept 2015: Harry is seen for the first time in an eye-catching, geometric-patterned Gucci suit, designed by Alessandro Michele, when he attends a fashion event at a private members' club in Mayfair.

Oct 2015: The last One Direction concert before the group's hiatus is at the Motorpoint Arena, Sheffield.

Nov 2015: Wears an even bolder floral Gucci suit to the American Music Awards in Los Angeles. With longer rock-star hair, he stands out and apart from the rest of the group. The band wins Artist of the Year for the second time and performs 'Perfect', a track from their fifth and last album to date, *Made in the AM*.

Dec 2015: Fittingly, their last appearance on UK television is at the grand final of *The X Factor*. In the US they sing five songs on Carpool Karaoke with James Corden. The video has been watched nearly 184 million times on YouTube.

March 2016: Harry is the first big signing of Jeffrey Azoff's new company Full Stop Management. In a busy start to the year, he has already joined the Creative Artists Agency (CAA) and auditioned for a role in the World War II drama *Dunkirk*, directed by Christopher Nolan, who says Harry has an 'old-fashioned face'.

May 2016: Harry starts his own label, Erskine Records, an imprint that will release his records under the Columbia umbrella. His personal assistant, Emma Spring, is registered as company director.

July 2016: Begins filming his role as young soldier Alex, after two weeks of training in Northern France, swimming while wearing an overcoat with a pack on his back. His first line in a movie is, 'What's wrong with your friend?'

Dec 2016: Finishes most of his debut solo album at a villa and studio at Port Antonio in Jamaica with his new musical entourage, which includes guitarist Mitch Rowland – who was working in a pizza restaurant in Hollywood when he was asked to play at a recording session for Harry. They become great friends and collaborators.

Feb 2017: Columbia Records, which had been the US label of One Direction, confirm they will be releasing Harry's first solo album, *Harry Styles*. He is the only member of the band they sign.

April 2017: His debut solo single 'Sign of the Times' is heard for the first time on Nick Grimshaw's breakfast programme on Radio 1. The six-minute epic had been written in three hours after lunch in Jamaica when Harry started tinkering around on the piano. The song, a thoughtful commentary on the things that matter in the world, goes straight to number one in the UK. In the US, he appears on *Saturday Night Live* and does a hilarious impression of Mick Jagger.

May 2017: The album *Harry Styles* debuts at number one on both sides of the Atlantic and sells more than one million copies by the end of the year. His favourite track is 'From the Dining Table' because 'it's the most personal'. Performs with the legendary Stevie Nicks at the Troubadour, Los Angeles.

June 2017: Harry's stepfather Robin Twist dies aged 57 after a long battle with cancer. Niall Horan describes him as 'the nicest, kindest, most generous, hilariously funny guy you'll have met'.

July 2017: Attends the premiere of *Dunkirk* at the Odeon, Leicester Square, and chats backstage to Prince Harry, who is guest of honour. The movie makes $527 million at the box office.

Sept 2017: Waves a rainbow flag that a member of the audience threw onto the stage at the first *Live on Tour* concert in San Francisco. The LGBTQ+ Pride symbol would become a fixture at his shows. After the concert in LA, he goes out for sushi with his girlfriend, the model Camille Rowe. Writes 'Watermelon Sugar' during a break before his show in Nashville.

March 2018: Tweets in support of the March for Our Lives, the youth-led protest in Washington urging gun control. Camille is seen dancing next to his mum Anne at his Paris concert.

June 2018: He begins Pride month by announcing that the proceeds from a special-edition Treat People with Kindness t-shirt would go to GLSEN (Gay, Lesbian and Straight Education Network), which champions inclusive and safe school environments. Dances with a rainbow flag and a Black Lives Matter flag at his concerts in New York and Chicago.

March 2019: Harry gives the presentation speech in New York in honour of Stevie Nicks when she becomes the only woman to be inducted twice into the Rock and Roll Hall of Fame. They sing a duet of her classic song 'Don't Go Draggin' My Heart Around'.

May 2019: It's a big night for Harry when he is co-host for the famous Met Gala (Met Ball) in New York. The theme of the evening is 'Camp: Notes on Fashion'. Pictures of Harry in a Gucci sheer-black ruffled top with a lace bib go round the world.

Oct 2019: 'Lights Up', the lead single from his second album, is released. While it doesn't reach number one in the US or the UK, the steamy video filmed in Mexico is watched 95 million times. Harry gives evidence behind a screen at Hendon Magistrates Court in North London in a harassment case involving a stalker who had been camped outside his home for months, leaving him 'scared and very uncomfortable'.

Nov 2019: Hosts *Saturday Night Live* in New York and reveals comic talent in a series of sketches including playing a Chihuahua. Show regular Cecily Strong calls his performance 'magical'. Announces *Love on Tour* promoting his album *Fine Line* will begin in Birmingham in April 2020.

Dec 2019: Harry steps in to host *The Late Late Show* in Los Angeles when his friend James Corden dashes off to be with his wife Julia, who is about to give birth. Plays a game of Spill Your Guts or Fill Your Guts with Kendall Jenner. Harry becomes the first UK male artist to have his two albums debut at number one in the US when *Fine Line* reaches the top. Plays a secret gig at the Electric Ballroom in Camden with Stormzy as the special guest.

Jan 2020: Enjoys a Caribbean holiday with friends including Adele and James Corden. Harry and Adele leave their waiter a timely tip of $2,020 (£1,500) at a seafood restaurant in the Virgin Islands and scribble 'Happy New Year' on the receipt.

Feb 2020: Harry is mugged at knifepoint near his London home. Caroline Flack is found dead and Harry wears a simple black ribbon on his Gucci suit at the BRIT Awards in her memory. He performs 'Falling', a moving ballad from the album about his relationship with ex-girlfriend Camille Rowe.

March 2020: Announces postponement of *Love on Tour* owing to Covid-19.

May 2020: Five days after the murder of George Floyd, Harry posts on Twitter, 'Being not racist is not enough. We must be anti-racist.'

June 2020: Takes part in a peaceful Black Lives Matter protest through the streets of Hollywood.

July 2020: Harry tweets on the tenth anniversary of the formation of One Direction. He thanks everyone who helped the band along the way and says, 'To all the fans, I love you and I thank you with all my heart.' His comments are liked more than 10.5 million times.

Aug 2020: 'Watermelon Sugar' finally becomes his first US number one single.

Sept 2020: Harry is cast opposite Florence Pugh as a 1950s husband in the new psychological thriller *Don't Worry Darling*, directed by Olivia Wilde, one of Hollywood's most prominent activists and feminists. He replaces Shia LaBeouf, who, it's alleged, had been fired by Olivia for his poor behaviour on set. She does a 'little victory dance' when Harry agrees to step up.

Dec 2020: Harry becomes the first solo man to appear on the cover of *Vogue*. He is wearing a sky-blue, lace, Gucci ballgown that reaches to the floor and a black Gucci tuxedo jacket. He breaks the internet. He is recognised as the most popular UK celebrity on Twitter with 35.7 million (and rising) followers. He has even more on Instagram – 39 million.

Jan 2021: Releases video for 'Treat People with Kindness' that features him dancing with Phoebe Waller-Bridge in the manner of an old-fashioned Hollywood musical. The world realises Harry and Olivia are a couple when they arrive holding hands at the wedding of Jeffrey Azoff in Montecito, California. Olivia had split from her long-term partner and father of her two children, Jason Sudeikis, in November.

March 2021: Wins first Grammy, claiming Best Pop Solo Performance for 'Watermelon Sugar'. Spends the early summer in London filming *My Policeman*, again set in the 1950s, in which he co-stars with Emma Corrin.

May 2021: Takes a break from filming scenes in Brighton to collect BRIT Award for Best British Single for 'Watermelon Sugar.' Fans are bemused by his semi-American accent when he gives his thanks on stage. The *Sunday Times* Rich List puts his wealth at £75 million, an annual rise of £12 million.

June 2021: *My Policeman* wraps in Venice. Harry and Olivia begin a romantic break in Tuscany before flying back to the US, where he starts rehearsals for his live concerts.

Aug 2021: Harry's beloved grandfather, Brian Selley, dies after suffering from Parkinson's disease for many years. His heartbroken mum praises her 'brave and courageous' father.

Sept 2021: *Love on Tour* finally gets under way in Las Vegas. Olivia is there supporting him and the Pride flag is back. In a rare tweet, Harry says, 'Vegas, you blew me away. I'd been waiting for that. Thank you so much for all the love. I had the time of my life with you. H.'

ACKNOWLEDGEMENTS

As this is a book about Harry Styles, I thought I would start with fashion and specifically thank Alison Jane Reed, who has helped me countless times over the years. She is a very talented writer on many subjects, as well as fashion. She has just started *The Luminaries Magazine* online and I am so jealous! She describes it as 'The Organic Arts, Entertainment, Food and Fashion Magazine: Inspiring You to Live Well and Make a Difference Through the Power of Journalism and Storytelling.' It's well worth checking out at theluminariesmagazine.com.

AJ, as her friends know her, loved looking at Harry and his fashion development over the years. She is hoping he doesn't take any period film roles for a while so he can grow his 'wonderful hair' again because it looks so good with a flower-power Gucci suit.

Many thanks as always to Gordon Wise, my agent at Curtis Brown, who continues to look after my interests so well. Next year we will be having a celebratory lunch to mark fifteen years since I was lucky enough to be taken on as a client; his assistant Niall Harman has once more been a terrific help, especially during such a difficult working year for everyone.

That's also true of everyone at HarperCollins. I don't know how they have managed to get the books out this year, so nice one you guys. Thanks in particular to Kelly Ellis for commissioning *Harry Styles: The Making of a Modern Man* and her Desk Editor, Holly Blood, for making sure everything ran smoothly day to day. Thanks also to Georgina Atsiaris, Senior Project Editor; Sarah Burke, Senior Production Controller; Fiona Greenway, Picture Research; Mark Rowland, Designer; Claire Ward, Creative Director; Hattie Evans, Marketing Executive; Anni Shaw, Press Officer; Tom Dunston, Sales Director; Alice Gomer, Head of International Sales; Zoe Shine, Head of UK Rights; and Fionnuala Barrett, Audio Editorial Director.

I've been so lucky to have Helena Caldon looking after the words. As well as being a superb copy editor, she went to see Harry Styles' secret Christmas gig at the Electric Ballroom, Camden, in 2019. I wish I'd been there!

I am grateful to Jo Westaway, who once more has helped me with all things online and technical. She is now in her second year of a master's degree in singing at the Royal Welsh College of Music & Drama. The pandemic has made it a tricky time for the acting profession but it's been my good fortune to secure Eleanor Williams as my chief researcher for this book. I hope things are picking up for talented actors now, although I hope she will still have the time to help with my next book. Thanks also to Jen Westaway for transcribing my interviews again and to Madeleine Moore for another fascinating star chart. She is a fixture in all of my books and I urge you to take a look even if you are not particularly interested in the world of astrology. You will be after reading 'Harry's Stars'. I have been fortunate to have the help of PJ Norman at AuthorProfile (www.authorprofile.co.uk) in guiding me through the digital possibilities for my books.

I really enjoyed my trip up to Harry's home patch, Holmes Chapel in Cheshire. I had never been there before. Everyone was charming. I kept on meeting people who had been to the local comprehensive school too, which was a bonus. And of course I had to sample an ice cream from the Great Budworth Ice Cream Farm and a bun from the W. Manderley Bakery. I met a lady there who had once been sold double-glazing by Robbie Williams. What a small world! I wrote about Rob a few years ago and remembered that was his job when he left school. And I had a pint (or two) in the Antrobus Arms where Harry lived at one time as a boy, as well as sweet and sour from the Chinese take-away a few doors down from his home. I love travelling to the places where dreams begin.

Finally, a word for the Harry Styles fans: I hope you enjoy this look at your hero. He is a fascinating, interesting man and I hope I have done him justice. I would like to give a special thank you to Millie Caldon, a devoted Harry fan who has read every word of this book and made sure I stayed on the right track.

You can read more about my books at seansmithceleb.com or follow me on Twitter or Facebook @seansmithceleb.

SELECT BIBLIOGRAPHY

Cowen, Elle, *Harry Styles Photo-Biography*, Plexus, 2013

Flack, Caroline, *Storm in a C Cup*, Simon & Schuster UK, 2015

Jepson, Louisa, *Every Piece of Me*, Simon & Schuster UK, 2013

One Direction, *Dare to Dream*, HarperCollins, 2011

One Direction, *Where We Are*, HarperCollins, 2013

Smith, Sean, *Ed Sheeran*, HarperCollins, 2018

PICTURE CREDITS

INDEX